AN EXAMINATION OF CHILD PSYCHOLOGY

EDWARD GLOVER (London)

I. *Introductory.*

II. *The Development of Child-Analysis.*

III. *Outline of Kleinian Theories.*
    (a) *The First Phase.*
    (b) *The Second Phase.*

IV. *The New Kleinian Metapsychology.*
    (a) *The Kleinian Concept of Phantasy.*
    (b) *Introjection and Projection.*
    (c) *The Kleinian Conception of Regression.*
    (d *The 'Depressive Position.'*

V. *Conclusion.*

I
INTRODUCTORY.

During the last twenty years the development of a specialised branch of child analysis has brought to a head a number of controversial issues the solution of which will influence analytical theory for some time to come. It was of course inevitable that clinical psycho-analysts should, sooner or later, begin to "specialise" in various branches of morbid psychology, thereby following the example of earlier colleagues who had "specialised" in different fields of applied psycho-analysis—anthropology, literature, folk-lore and the like. Indeed it is more than probable that as our knowledge of different varieties of mental disorder increases it will not be possible for the "general practitioner in psycho-analysis" to be equally competent in all branches of psychopathology. The apparent "all-round" ability he exhibits at present depends on the fact that our knowledge regarding the development of most psycho-pathological states though accurate enough is still rudimentary. Transference and other factors of technique apart, therapeutic results depend on the extent to which we apply sound analytical understanding; and we have just enough understanding of the main mental mechanisms common to all cases to produce some beneficial results. Up to the present at any rate there is no evidence that etiological fads or special systems of interpretation have any outstanding therapeutic virtue, still less that these isolated systems can be made the basis of a new metapsychology.

However that may be, it is interesting to note that the first sign of clinical specialisation in psycho-analysis was the development of a branch of child-analysis, a division which in course of time was reflected in the organisation of psycho-analytical clinics. Child-departments, sometimes, as in the case of the London Clinic of Psycho-analysis, of an extremely nebulous character, made an arbitary distinction between child-analysts and other analytical practitioners more marked. Naturally this was followed by a clinically unjustified acquisition of prestige on the part of child-analysts, and to this prestige factor together with an outbreak of inferiority feeling on the part of ordinary analysts, I attribute some of the chaos that has recently arisen in psycho-analytical circles in Britain. The assumption of prestige is based on the unwarranted view that because children are passing through an important stage of mental development, this fact somehow or other gives the analytical observer more ready contact with unconscious mental processes. This assumption soon gives rise to a vicious circular argument. I have heard child analysts base their theoretical views on their observations of children and subsequently maintain the accuracy of their observations on the strength of their interpretations. Left unchecked this process can have only one result, a quite unjustified arrogation of authority by child-analysts over the theoretical and technical development of psycho-analysis*. By way of illustration one might quote the view of some British analysts that the age-limit for a child-analysis department and for the application of child techniques should be not less than 18 years and preferably 21, an age which our grandmothers often celebrated by the birth of their first child. No doubt administrative follies of this sort are not hard to correct: patients themselves will in any case see to that. Much more difficult to offset is the influence of theoretical conceptions put forward by certain child-analysts or groups of child-analysts. The present paper is intended to examine the views and theories put forward by the Klein Group of the British Psycho-Analytical Society.

---

* A similar situation threatens to develop regarding the importance of psychiatry to psycho-analysis. The fact that the regressions, restitutive symptom-formations and disintegration products observed in the psychoses are of a primitive type tends to give the observer the impression that he is in specially close touch with unconscious mental processes, and encourages him in the belief that he may speak with special authority on psycho-analytical matters. Whereas the plain fact is that up to the present the study of psychoses remains for the largest part an observational field in which the essential techniques of psycho-analytical research are almost as limited in application as they are in the study of early infancy.

II
THE DEVELOPMENT OF CHILD-ANALYSIS.

Elsewhere in this volume W. Hoffer has examined in some detail the general development of child psycho-analysis but before investigating the Kleinian system, which in my opinion constitutes a deviation from accepted Freudian metapsychology, it is necessary to review briefly the part played by the psycho-analysis of children in the development of psycho-analytical theory. Up to the time when Kleinian views first obtained currency amongst a small group in the British Society, child-analysts in the real sense of the term (i.e. practitioners who devote their energies almost exclusively to the actual psycho-analysis of children up to the age of puberty) were few and far between. Psycho-analytically trained observers of children were common enough. Most practising psycho-analysts had been at one time or other at pains to collect observations of child behaviour and to adduce these in confirmation of already established psycho-analytic findings. In short, child-analysis was in the first instance a branch of applied psycho-analysis, a behavouristic study similar to the analytic study of the psychoses or of the behaviour and ideologies of primitive races. Indeed as far as infancy is concerned it must remain an observational study, for until the child's mind has reached the stage of development at which it can apprehend the meaning of interpretations (even if these were made by dumb show) the psychic situation between the child and the analyst remains one of spontaneous or at the most developed rapport only: no true "analytical situation" can exist.[*] However much the observer may be oriented in psycho-analysis, theories of development advanced on the strength of observations only, are, at best, plausible reconstructions and, at worst, subjective phantasies.

Nevertheless it is significant that some of the most important early advances in psycho-analysis arose from a psychic situation in which indirect observation was combined with vicarious interpretation. It is scarcely necessary to remind readers that Freud's analysis of Little Hans resulted not only in a classical outline of the Oedipus situation but in increased understanding of the dynamics of the unconscious mind and in particular of the role of anxiety and repression during that classical phase. As was only natural the work of the early child analysts (Hug-Helmuth, Pfister, etc.) reflected with some fidelity the existing state of psycho-analytical theory. So close was the correspondence, that it would not be unfair to say that the findings of the early child analysts were more corroborative than original in scope. They confirmed what psycho-analysis and analytical observation of adults had led Freud to infer regarding the unconscious mind of the child. And to a very considerable extent this has remained the case down to the present time. As Freud step by step expanded our knowledge of the structure and function of the unconscious mind, child analysts vied with analytical anthropologists and analytical psychiatrists to confirm his findings in their respective fields. This was at the same

---

[*] As a matter of fact even if Klein's entire system were sound, i.e., if the infant a few months after birth possessed a psychic apparatus already differentiated into ego and super-ego, capable of the elaborate and sophisticated system of unconscious and pre-conscious phantasy Klein describes, and, *a priori* capable of developing a classical transference neurosis, this would still not justify the assumption that an "analytic situation" is possible. Neither the transference nor its associated resistance could be analysed until their meaning could be conveyed.

time a tribute to the amazing accuracy of Freud's observations and a step towards that corroboration which is necessary for the acceptance of analytical theories. But apart from filling in a few gaps here and there and from producing clinical illustrations from normal and abnormal children, all the more fascinating because they were observations made during actual analysis of children, it could not be said that child analysts had contributed much to the expansion of analytic theory.

Of course the lines of research were obvious enough. Freud had mapped out both positive and negative aspects of the Oedipus situation, and had later outlined the structure of the mind at that phase. By his analysis of obsessional neurosis in particular he had been able to thrust deeply into the stage immediately preceding the Oedipus phase. But between that pre-Oedipus phase and the earliest phases of infantile psychic activity, which perforce were only understood in terms of hypothetical reconstruction, a gap remained only slenderly bridged by delineation of "stages in the development of the libido", by conceptions of the development of object relationship ("auto-erotism"—narcissism"—"object-choice"), and by etiological formulations regarding paranoia and melancholia. All these were expressed mainly in terms of libidinal development, although the use of phrases such as "oral-sadism," "anal-sadism," "ambivalence" and the like shewed an understanding of the part played by impulses of aggression and attitudes of hate which were only later formulated by Freud with more precision. Not only was there a gap between hypothetical reconstructions of early mental function and clinical outlines of the mind at the Oedipus phase, there were in existence no cross sections of the mind during the pre-oedipus phases comparable with the cross sections Freud had made for 3-5 year old children. Concepts of Ego, Superego and Id for example, were first mapped out in terms of the classical Oedipus phase. Pre-oedipus regulator systems in the ego (concepts so essential to psycho-analytical psychology) were not described. Ferenczi combining the concept of the anal-sadistic stage of the libido with that of the super-ego had shot his bolt by describing "Sphinkter moral," but although suggestive enough in theory and useful enough in practice, this formulation was not sufficiently correlated with ego-structure. The sign posts to research could not be mistaken. Advances had to be made from two directions, from the clinical end where actual analysis could be effected, and from the "reconstruction" end. It was a task which incidentally called for close correlation of effort in every branch of psycho-analysis. But above all it called for original work on the part of child analysts.

The dangers inherent in this situation were equally obvious. Hypothetical reconstructions of the mind in early infancy, however far they may be extended, can never meet and link up with clinical observations. They are of a different order. They can increase the plausibility of a clinical interpretation, and their own plausibility can be reinforced by clinical interpretations. But they cannot really dovetail with clinical facts. Attempts to merge them usually lead to the confusion that so often follows the blending of subjective phantasy with scientific fact. There are of course some exceptions to this rule. Freud himself provided one of the most distinguished exceptions to it. But he never confused hypothesis with facts. In less skilled hands the method results in absurdity. It was indeed this importation of absurdity into Freud's metapsychology that was finally responsible for the reaction against the later stage of Kleinian theory.

III
OUTLINE OF KLEINIAN THEORIES.

I mention this fact because it is essential to understand that Kleinian theories fall into two phases. The first of these ended for all practical purposes with the appearance of her book "The Psycho-Analysis of Children" in 1932, the second began with the publication of her paper on depression in 1934. The fact that there are two distinct phases of Kleinian theory is not sufficiently recognised and in consequence there has been a good deal of confusion of allegiance in the British Society. Some members who favoured views put forward by Melanie Klein in her "first phase" have unthinkingly supported the theories produced in the "second phase". They were evidently under the misapprehension that the latter were mere logical extensions of earlier views. Admittedly there is some ideological continuity between the two phases, and it is not difficult to find in the earlier phase many of the confusions of thought and terminology which later on were developed into a heterodox brand of metapsychology. But the two phases are otherwise quite distinct. Klein's earliest theories constituted an attempt to fill in the gap I have described above: her later formulations, starting from the assumption of a "central depression position" said to be characteristic of all mental development, are of a much more ambitious order. If accepted they would involve a complete recasting of our accepted ideas of mental development : *if they are inaccurate, and that is the main contention of this paper, they represent a major deviation from psycho-analytical principles.*

(a) *The First Phase.* Melanie Klein's book, "The Psycho-Analysis of Children" was an expansion of two courses of lectures interspersed with a few chapters based on earlier papers on the subject. There is consequently a good deal of overlapping and repetition of argument but the main outline is as follows :—

> From the middle of the first year onward the oral frustrations of the child, together with increase of its oral sadism, release Oedipus impulses. The super-ego begins to develop at the same time. The immediate consequence of oral frustration is the desire to "incorporate" the father's penis. But this is accompanied by the theory that the mother " incorporates " and retains possession of the father's penis. The impulse is then aroused to destroy in various primitive ways the mother's body and its contents. In the case of the girl the impulse to destroy the mother's body gives rise to a danger situation equivalent to the castration anxiety of the boy, viz., fear of destruction of her own body. Incidentally, it is laid down that anxiety springs from aggression. As soon as the child's process of " incorporation " has begun, the incorporated object becomes the vehicle of defence against the destructive impulses in the organism. The child is afraid of being exterminated by its destructive impulses and projects them on an external object which it then tries to destroy by oral-sadistic means. And this in turn involves incorporating a " bad " object which acts as a severe super-ego. This primary defence by oral aggression soon extends to urethral and anal-sadistic systems. These all turn in the first place against the mother's breast, but later against other, sometimes corresponding, parts of the mother's body. These primary

defences continue unabated until the decline of the earlier anal-sadistic stage. Oral frustration also arouses an unconscious knowledge that the parents enjoy mutual sexual pleasures (at first thought of in oral terms), and the oral envy aroused makes the child wish to push into the mother's body, and is at the same time responsible for its epistemophilic trends. These phantasied attacks are directed in particular at the orally incorporated penis of the father. The boy, for example, is ultimately afraid of the mother's body because it contains the father's penis, i.e., fear tends to be displaced from the penis to the body. The most anxiety-provoking situation is that where the mother's possession of the father's penis is regarded by the child as combination against him of both father and mother.

With the boy, Oedipus conflict sets in with hatred of the father's penis in the mother's body and desire for genital union with the mother. The girl in her anxiety, turns from the mother (body) to the father (penis). In both, the impulses of hate bring about the Oedipus situation and the formation of the super-ego. It is clearly laid down that the child's earliest identifications should be called a super-ego. This institution helps to overcome anxiety and sadism, but of course anxiety itself is partly responsible for the expansion of different erotogenic interests. The child's introjected objects (which are essentially organ-objects) exercise a phantastic severity and therefore arouse intense anxiety. Indeed, in the early anal-sadistic phase the child is trying to "eject his super-ego," and not only his super-ego but his Id. Up to the end of this phase we have all the fixation points for the psychoses. The processes of introjection and projection are reciprocal, and during these phases the ego deals with objects as the super-ego deals with the ego and as the ego deals with the super-ego and Id. This introduces a confusion between the phantasied and the reality dangers of the object. The " real " object contributes a little, but as a rule only a little to this anxiety situation. The child's original hate of the object is reinforced by hate of the super-ego and Id.

Modification of these early anxieties and defences is effected through the libido and through relations to real objects. Even the earliest turning from the mother's breast to the father's penis is a libidinal step forward from an anxiety situation, although not at first a very succesful step. In the girl it is the precursor of the Oedipus situation; in the boy it may, unless overcome by a second orientation to the mother, leads to a deep homosexual fixation on the father. What we call stages in the development of the libido really represent positions won by the libido in its struggle with destructive impulses. Moreover, suspicions regarding the external world evoked by projecting sadism on to it lead to a closer contact with real objects. These factors, following the process of ejecting the destructive super-ego, prepare the way for more successful introjection of " good " objects. The new introjections lead in turn to modifications of the earliest anxiety phobias which are of a projective, paranoidal nature. In the later anal stage, when the super-ego begins to be "retained," anxiety develops into guilt, and obsessional features make their appearance. Ceremonials of object-restoration are a prominent feature at this stage, and are characterised by a belief in creative omnipotence which is necessary to counteract the belief in destructive (excretory) omnipotence. These obsessional symptoms are also a defence against early masturbatory systems, which themselves represent attempts to side-track sadistic Oedipus content. To these " pathological " measures of defence are added the more " normal" mechanisms of play, and of curiosity (search for knowledge) which serve to allay fears in the outer world. An attempt is now made to approximate the super-ego to real objects, and to build up a realistic ego-ideal system. The development of the super-ego and of the libido cease at the onset of the latency period. In general, differences in the super-ego structure of the boy and girl relate to differences in the history of aggressive and libidinal development. The girl's Oedipus phase is ushered in by oral desires for the father's penis which is thought to be in the mother's body. Her omnipotence then makes the girl believe that she has herself " incorporated " this penis. This reinforced incorporation tendency gives the girl a more powerful super-ego. Differences in the method of dealing with this "bad" introjected penis are responsible for differences in type observable amongst women. The girl's super-ego is also affected by ideas of sadistic omnipotence of excreta. And owing to the absence of the real penis she has more uncertainty about the inside of her body. In general, the girl's super-ego is more extensive than the boy's owing to the receptive nature of her impulses. The boy's primary omnipotence relates more to the possession of a real penis and less to the existence of an introjected father's penis. The girl introjects more than does the boy; she " needs " objects more, and is left ultimately with a more exalted super-ego. The boy in his original relation to the father's penis inside the mother's body concentrates more on destruction of the penis. In any case the stage of attack on the mother's body does not last so long as in the girl; moreover, the accompanying omnipotence is less excretory and more penile. Believing in the sadistic omnipotence of the penis, the boy concentrates on attacking the father's penis, and this leads to genital desires for the mother. When this penis-hate is displaced to the real penis of the father, typical castration anxiety develops.

Reviewing a book which sets out to describe in psycho-analytical terms the development of mind from the middle of the first year down to the latency period it is essential to keep the following questions clearly in mind (a) to what extent has the author drawn on accepted Freudian findings; (b) to what extent are any new formulations either in the nature of hypothetical reconstructions or direct analytical interpretations of a given period of development; (c) how far are the new formulations either accurate or plausible. And these test questions raise a number of other issues, e.g., what was the age of the children under analytical observation, how far is the reconstruction concerned with phantasies alleged to exist in the child's unconscious (and interpreted by the author) or on self-interpreting material, finally in the case of children of the age period 3-5, by what criteria are the alleged stages of earlier development established, and in particular how does the author distinguish between, on the one hand, products of fixation and regression, and on the other, current unconscious phantasies stimulated by the current psychological situation. Following these lines of approach it is possible to disentangle from a rather matted narrative the main outlines of early

Kleinian theory.

At a first reading one is apt to become confused by the fact that although the author gives an adequate list of references to the work of Freud, Abraham, Ferenczi, Jones and others, it is not always easy to indicate the point at which she gives their ideas her own particular twist. For instance, she constantly lays stress on the view that early anxieties are reduced by exploitation of libidinal phases. Now this is not an original discovery. Neither is the companion view that sadism (or rather the impulses of destruction and mastery) is a determining factor in mental conflict. To Freud himself, and later to Jones and Abraham, is due the credit of first describing the fundamental conception of ambivalence in comprehensive terms. Indeed it was unfortunate that the author did not preserve the strict connotation of this term, for throughout her book, the term " sadism " becomes a catchword. Melanie Klein was evidently caught up in the swing of the analytical pendulum from purely libidinal etiologies and soon landed herself in theories that aggression causes anxiety and that anxiety can be credited with the calling out of different libidinal phases. *Thus according to her impulses of hate bring about the Oedipus situation and stages in the development of the libido really represent positions won by the libido in its struggle with destructive impulses.* Possibly the author in formulating this sweeping hypothesis was biased by clinical observations made by Freud on homosexuality in particular that an earlier ambivalence or rivalry can be covered by a later homosexual attachment. But the generalisation she puts forward is not supported by direct analysis of a multiplicity of types of case, and in any event runs counter to all psycho-biological probability. Nevertheless the manner in which accepted Freudian views are interspersed with purely Kleinian hypotheses would lead the casual reader to imagine that the Kleinian conclusions arrived at are merely a logical extension of the more familiar Freudian premisses. Throughout the book it is essential to distinguish clearly what is accepted Freudian teaching and what is specifically a Kleinian accretion to it.

A second pitfall for the unwary reader is the fact that *the greater part of the author's description of mental development is purely hypothetical reconstruction.* This merges gradually with views based on her clinical analyses of children beyond the age of 3-4.* Of course, it can be argued that the child analyst is just as entitled to draw conclusions regarding the first two years of life from the analysis of 5-year-old children as the ordinary analyst is entitled to draw conclusions regarding the unconscious content of 5-year-old children from the analysis of adults. This argument is not valid. Not only are conclusions drawn from adult cases based on observations of every variety of case, but they can be confirmed by actual analysis of 5-year-olds. The assumptions made about early infancy cannot be confirmed by direct analysis and must remain reconstructions to be judged by their plausibility. Naturally the same applies to what are alleged to be the unconscious phantasies of the young infant. Yet the merging of these alleged early phantasies with later phantasy systems (whether the latter are accurately analysed or not) gives the former an air of objective

---

* From the age-table given by the author it appears that as far as the analysis of young children is concerned, her findings were based on the analysis of seven cases. The two youngest were 2¾ years and 3¼ years respectively: the other five varied from 3¾-5 years (average 4¼ years): all were diagnosed as severely neurotic: one exhibited psychotic traits. Of the others, five were in the latency period (variation 6-9): two pre-pubertal (9½) and four pubertal (12-14): one adult case is included.

observation which is likely to lead the reader astray. This is best illustrated by the conclusions regarding the Oedipus complex arrived at by the author. Melanie Klein holds that owing to oral frustration the Oedipus complex is released at the middle of the first year. The sadism engendered by this frustration activates the Oedipus situation. Now it has frequently been reported that infants from the age of six to eighteen months show *larval* genital reactions, and these observations have gained strength from the fact that genital excitation can be observed in small babies. These are interesting observations, but they do not permit generalisations about the universality of an " Oedipus complex" existing from the 6th month of life, and they certainly do not constitute proof that even in the cases described by Melaine Klein the sequence of events described by her is valid. The accepted theory of primacy of different libidinal components at different stages of development does not exclude the existence of genital elements at an early stage and, as Freud was ready to concede, there is no objection to calling all pregenital relations between the infant and its parent Oedipus relations. But that is not Melanie Klein's point. She states specifically that phantasies concerning the father's penis (inside the mother) follow immediately on oral frustration, hence that her " first year Oedipus situation " is a true genital Oedipus situation. Putting aside for the moment the question whether phantasies exist at this stage, it will be seen that Melanie Klein whilst at some points accepting both explicitly and implicity the concept of libidinal primacies, in effect undercuts the significance of later infantile genital primacy. No doubt the depth of true genital Oedipus systems had previously been underestimated. Whether the author's conclusions are right or wrong, there can be no doubt that they led to a broader conception of the Oedipus phase. *The fact remains however that her own descriptions of the course of events are purely hypothetical and lack the clinical backing by which the classical Freudian views are supported.* The Freudian view is that the Oedipus situation results from an infantile genital (phallic) primacy occurring at a phase when the ego is definitely organised and about to undergo its final differentiation. I have every sympathy with the desire to trace genital elements in the primitive and unorganised ego : and in fact I have myself postulated primitive genital (nuclear) formations in early infancy, but that is not the same thing as postulating an active Oedipus situation. Moreover, the Freudian position regarding the classical Oedipus situation is firmly based on analytic investigations. Melanie Klein's theories as to the onset of the Oedipus complex, the mechanisms which activate it, and the unconscious phantasies that precede that activation remains purely hypothetical and incapable of direct confirmation. Indeed it is difficult to escape the conclusion that Melanie Klein's " discovery " of the first year Oedipus complex was little more than a " hunch " based on the conviction that as infants undoubtedly possess some genital libido, there *must* be an Oedipus situation at an early stage. "Hunches" of this sort should not however be made the basis of dogmatic clinical formulations.

Concerning the early formation of the super-ego practically identical arguments are applicable. As I have pointed out earlier the question of " forerunners " of the super-ego, an institution which, according to accepted Freudian theory, is specifically connected with the disintegration of the Oedipus situation, has long exercised the minds of analytical investigators. But even in the field of hypothetical reconstruction, few attempts were made to describe the regulator systems of the primitive ego. In the early days of super-ego controversy critics used to take rather easily for granted that anything preceding the end of the phallic phase should be regarded as belonging to the stage of a " primitive Ego " which was supposéd partly to obey and partly to project the urgencies of the Id. But although I was among the first to support Melanie Klein's view that true super-ego formation occurs earlier than had previously been supposed, I expressed the opinion that the earliest super-ego formations she outlined could be better described as forerunners of the super-ego—that is to say as differentiations in the primitive ego brought about by the action of primitive mechanisms during the earlier phases of reality-proving. In principle, of course, any psychic imprint which is sufficiently permanent, and which leads to the subdivision of instinctual energies within the ego (Freud's "turning on the self ") can be regarded as having super-ego characteristics in the sense that however rudimentary the formation may be, it functions dynamically in the same way as the super-ego proper. And I think it is probable that as the earlier components of infantile sexuality lose their respective primacies and together with their associated reactive (sadistic or aggressive) drives fall before the action of repression, these primitive traces of ego-regulator systems become more organised and finally form substantial systems on which the super-ego proper is superimposed. Elsewhere I have put forward a " nuclear theory " of ego development which I believe meets many of the difficulties in reconstructing these earlier stages of ego development and differentiation. But these attempts belong mainly to the field of hypothetical reconstruction and are capable of clinical corroboration only in so far as the later pre-Oedipus phases are concerned. Obviously, however early rudiments of super-ego systems may make their appearance, the lines of demarcation between the Id, (?) primitive ego nuclei and (?) primitive super-ego nuclei can never be very clear. It may be that structural analogies are less useful in describing the early psyche than estimations of function in terms of energy, i.e., the quantities of unmodified instinct passing through a psychic system.

This, as I have said, is legitimate speculation. All we can say with certainty is that there is a good case for postulating earlier forms of super-ego. But it is one thing to outline hypothetical systems and quite another to affirm as Melaine Klein has done the actual existence of an super-ego based in the development of an Oedipus situation at the sixth month of life. She maintains that the child, being afraid of being exterminated by its destructive impulses, projects them on an external object which it then tries to destroy by oral-sadistic means and that this in turn involves " incorporating " a " bad " object which acts as a severe super-ego. The incorporated object becomes the vehicle of defence against the destructive impulses in the organism. The incorporated object is, however, an " organ-object," e.g., the father's penis existing in the mother; and apparently this organ object, which when, incorporated, acts as a severe and destructive super-ego, can be "ejected." The description of the later stages follows the same lines: a series of unconscious phantasies is postulated and extended in terms more appropriate to the description of mental mechanisms. By creating this confusion of terms it is easy for the author to adduce the postulated phantasies as a proof of the existence of the super-ego. Admittedly it is always hard to prevent anthropomorphism from creeping into psychological terminology, but the liberties Melanie Klein takes with metapsychological terms lead to the creation of a kind of slang in which it is no longer possible to distinguish between mechanisms, psychic imprints (nuclei or institutions) and unconscious presentations (including phantasies). The advantages of a threefold approach to mind, dynamic, structural and topographic are sacrificed to a confused presentation of phantasy. The phrase " introjected penis " for example, is nothing more than a mixed metaphor. It is possible to maintain that the child unconsciously attributes psychic tension to the presence in its body of an imaginary penis or enemy. It can be maintained further that if the child unconsciously applies the mechanism of projection to the instinctual tension, he may then develop a new unconscious phantasy, namely, of ejecting the enemy from his body. But to talk of the child trying to eject the super ego is manifestly absurd. Confusions of this kind would soon reduce metapsychology to a farrago of nonsense.

It is important to keep this confusion in Kleinian thinking in mind, for, as will be seen later, the whole of her metapsychology is based on it. On the other hand, eliminate this confusion and the greater part of the Kleinian system disappears. *It becomes merely a postulated system of unconscious phantasies to which is attached a hypothetical reconstruction of the mind in early infancy.* Take, for example, comparisons of the super-ego in the boy and girl respectively. Discussions of psychological differences of this kind have always aroused a certain amount of heat in psycho-analytical circles. Many psycho-analytical writers have damaged their reputations in attempts to clarify the issue. And without doubt the problem will not be solved until more detailed researches have been carried out on pre-genital stages. Now Melanie Klein follows the perfectly legitimate assumption that many of the psychological differences between the sexes crystallise out in super-ego formations. But as the super-ego in her view is developed from the first year of life and stimulated by specific sets of alleged unconscious phantasy the validity of her differentiations depends finally on the accuracy of her reconstructions and interpretations. Unless her primary assumptions are correct the whole of her system falls to the ground.

Indeed this is the trouble with most of the formulations contained in the book. They depend on dogmatic assumptions regarding the psychic content of the first and second years of life, a period concerning which we know least. Stripped of their repetitions and overlappings, and deprived of their metapsychological expressions the phantasies she postulates are the sole basis of the Kleinian system. It is true the book contains many generalisations that are extremely plausible, but it is interesting to note that the most plausible of them do not depend on the accuracy or otherwise of her postulated phantasies. Some are in the nature of reasonable reflections about mental development. Thus, it is certainly plausible that the super-ego of the classical Oedipus phase has fore-runners. And it is one of Melanie Klein's services to psychoanalysis that her insistence on the point focussed attention on a comparatively neglected problem. Again, quite apart from the question of precocious or delayed development of the classical Oedipus complex, it is a reasonable assumption that earlier object relations with the parents constitute characteristic systems which are influenced by the primacy of certain unconscious mechanisms. Following Freud's views on the relation of the Super-ego to the Oedipus situation I have pointed out that the structure of the ego is inevitably influenced by *abandonment* of the object cathexes characteristic of any given primacy, and it is extremely probable that each ego modification contributes to the mastering of the anxieties of the period. Again it is reasonable to suppose that since in the later stages of development libido can be exploited to counter anxieties (of whatever origin) similar exploitations occur in earlier stages, and it is likely that the interaction of these various factors influences the modification of both libidinal and aggressive impulses, and so ultimately influences the processes of fixation and regression. It is also clear that the formation of object imagines must be influenced by projection which therefore plays a reflexive part in the formation of introjections. Melanie Klein certainly deserves credit for having brought these and other reflections to bear on problems of early development. No doubt it was for this reason that her earlier formulations became popular in the British Psycho-Analytical Society.

Unfortunately the author was not content with these legitimate inferences from accepted Freudian theories. In her eagerness to give a theoretical basis to the phantasy systems she had postulated, she did not hesitate to develop theories which deviated from fundamental Freudian concepts. In some cases the deviation is quite apparent as where she holds that libidinal positions or primacies are called out by struggles with the aggressive impulses. In others, the full implications of her views did not become clear until her " second stage " of theorising was reached. Thus, having stated that the alternation of processes of projection and introjection introduces a confusion between the phantasied and the reality dangers of the object, she goes on to affirm that the " real " object contributes a little, but as a rule only a little to this anxiety situation. It is instructive to compare this with Freud's categorical statement regarding the nature of anxiety in the last stage of infantile development, viz., " frightening *instinctual* situations can in the last resort be traced back to *external* situations of danger " adding that it is not the objective injury that is feared but a state of traumatic excitation " which cannot be dealt with in accordance with the norms of the pleasure principle."* By thus relating anxiety to a *factor in mental economy*, Freud not only gave a sound metapsychological basis to the theory of anxiety, but cut the ground, once and for all, from all attempts either to interpret all mental development in terms of one stage of it or to interpret all mental disorders in terms of one etiological formula. Again Klein's view that the earliest identifications of the child should be called a super-ego is convenient enough for her own theoretical purposes, but reduces our accepted ideas of egostructure to inextricable confusion.

It remains to consider how this first phase of Kleinian theory was received in psychoanalytical groups. This can be summed up by saying that in the British Society, Kleinian theories became quite a vogue, in the continental countries they were either rejected outright or treated with considerable reserve, whilst in the American Branch Societies they provoked no very definite reaction. The active support given in the British Society came mostly from pupil-followers, whose contributions however, did little more than echo the views of their teacher. There was, however, one important exception. Ernest Jones' papers on the " Phallic Phase " for example were based to a very considerable extent on Kleinian views regarding early development. At first no doubt a good deal of this support was due to dissatisfaction with the progress of

---

* New Introductory Lectures on Psycho-analysis." Hogarth Press, 1933.

psycho-analysis in mapping out early stages of development. This, together with the fact that Melanie Klein's views at first promised to extend our knowledge of these stages made the Society all the more ready to accept her formulations without too close scrutiny of their implications. And it seems likely that if the followers of Melanie Klein had not been so fervent in their adherence the exaggerations of her system would have been corrected by scientific discussion, and a useful residue might have remained. Indeed there is still in my opinion a useful residue to be extracted from this early phase of Kleinian theory. Unfortunately this process of extraction did not take place* Society discussions degenerated into the repetition of stereotyped Kleinian interpretations by which the distinctive outlines of different etiological formulae became blurred. In the meantime the unreflecting endorsement given by some members of the Society to Melanie Klein's earlier formulae was extended also to later expansions of these formulae. Gradually new ideas (expressed in discussions) on the nature of reality made it obvious that Kleinian views pushed to their logical conclusion would run counter to Freudian teaching on the early stages of Ego-development. Whether in the long run her earlier theories would have

* My own reactions to the new system were as follows: From the time I first published some observations on the oral phase of libido development (1924) my main theoretical and clinical interests were devoted to attempted reconstructions of early stages of ego-development, and to correlation of these stages with different forms of mental disorder. It had always appeared to me that until such correlations were made and distinctive etiological formulae established for different disorders, no important advances could be made in clinical psycho-analysis. When Melanie Klein first adumbrated her theories, I found them stimulating. As I have said many of her reflections appeared to me to be sound inferences from the works of Freud, Abraham and Ferenczi. Possibly the fact that like Melanie Klein I had been a pupil of Abraham made me more readily responsive to her general line of thought which both then and later was considerably influenced by Abraham's work. On the other hand I was always dubious about the validity of her phantasy interpretations. They were confused and tangled in content, and complicated to a degree that suggested the influence of preconscious elaboration on the part of their author. And at that time Melanie Klein had not produced any metapsychological formulations worthy of the name, although her tendency to make a goulasch of metapsychological terms in the process of describing unconscious-content was deplorably evident. It was clear however that her views would not be acceptable to what were called in this country " orthodox Freudians." And for a time I set myself the task of trying to find a compromise between Kleinian and Freudian concepts. This resulted in a paper given at the Oxford Congress (1929) entitled "Grades of Ego-differentiation."*(1)

Summing up the situation I expressed myself as follows:—" I believe that when all due corrections have been made the most important of Klein's findings will remain unchallenged, viz., the pre-phallic Oedipus phase, and the pregenital phase of super-ego formation. Even granting this, we are no better off as far as the primitive phases of the Ego are concerned. Indeed the tendency of her work is one of Super-ego aggrandisement at the expense of the primitive Ego." And again, " There would appear to be a certain overestimation of the ego in the customary teaching and under-estimation of the primitive Ego in Klein's teaching." My own main conclusion regarding the question of reality-proving was stated thus, " In the sense of organised reactive function we are entitled to say that a ' real '-ego system exists from shortly after birth.'

But, as is so often the case, these unsolicited attempts at compromise ended by wringing concessions from their own sponsor rather than from the opposing parties. Not recognising that her primary observations were speculative rather than clinical, I assumed that they were clinically valid. If this should seem to represent a deplorable slipshodness on my part I would remind the reader that at that time (1924-29) most analysts inclined to accept papers published in analytical journals at their face-value. For example, although in collaboration with James Glover I had examined and rejected Rank's birth-trauma theory of neurosogenesis, most analysts took Rank's theories on trust until Freud a few years later delivered the *coup de grace* in "Inhibitions, Symptoms and Anxiety." In fact for some years both in public and in private discussions I lent considerable support to some of Melanie Klein's general conclusions, and referred freely to them in a number of clinical and theoretical papers.

But as time went on it was impossible to keep my misgivings from creeping into public comment on her work. This was at first very guardedly expressed in a paper " The Therapeutic Effect of Inexact Interpretation.*(2)

By 1933 my misgivings took the form of explicit criticism; these were expressed in a review*(3) written for the *International Journal of Psycho-analysis* of Melanie Klein's book " The Psycho-analysis of Children." Even at this stage I paid tribute to the stimulus of her work in terms that were, I now recognise, unduly laudatory: nevertheless the review contained practically all the criticisms which I have so far presented in this present paper. But it was not until 1934 that, in a paper entitled "Some aspects of Psycho-analytical Research.*(4) I came into open opposition, stating roundly that existing research activities in the Society were being "frozen " by the propagation of dogmatic views on matters concerning which a completely open mind was essential.
(1)* I.J.P.-A , 1930: xi. 1.
(2)* I.J.P.-A., 1931: xii. 397.
(3)* I.J.P.-A., 1933: xiv. 119
(4)* Read at the British Psycho-analytical Society, October 3rd, 1934.

been scientifically sifted it is now impossible to say, for in 1934 the situation was altered dramatically. The " second phase " of Kleinian theory set in.

(b) *The Second Phase.* In her paper entitled " A Contribution to the Psycho-genesis of Manic Depressive States,"* Melanie Klein stated that in her opinion " the infantile depressive position is the central position of the child's development." Starting with a brief re-statement of some of her earlier views, particularly concerning the phase of maximal sadism (which she believes to occur towards the end of the first year of life), the importance of introjection and projection of good or bad (part) objects and of the denial of psychic reality, she stated that a " depressive position " develops at the stage of passing from " part-object " to " whole-object " relations . . . . " not till the object is loved *as a whole* can its loss be felt as a whole." At this point there is an increase in introjection processes in order that, amongst other reasons, the love-object may be preserved in safety inside oneself. There are, however, characteristic anxieties at this stage, in particular, " anxiety lest the object be destroyed in the process of introjection " and " as to the dangers which await the object inside." The situation that is " fundamental for the loss of the loved object " is when " the ego becomes fully identified with its good internalised objects and, at the same time, becomes aware of its own incapacity to protect and preserve them against the internalised persecuting objects and the id." The paranoid mechanisms of destroying objects (in particular " expulsion and projection ") persist, although in a lesser degree, but lose value because of the dread of expelling the *good* object along with the bad. " The ego makes greater use of introjection of the *good* object as a mechanism of defence. This is associated with another important mechanism, that of making reparation to the object." But " the ego cannot as yet believe enough in the benevolence of the object and in its own capacity to make restitution." Every access of hate or anxiety may temporarily abolish the differentiation between good and bad internal objects and this results in " loss of the loved object." The ego is " full of anxiety lest such objects should die." This represents a " disaster " caused by the child's sadism. In depression " the ego's hate of the id accounts even more for its unworthiness and despair than its reproaches against the object."

The paranoiac has also introjected a whole and real object, but has not been able to achieve a full identification with it. Suffering associated with the depressive position may thrust him back on the paranoid position which can then be reinforced as a defence. The depressive state is genetically derived from the paranoid state. Another variety of defence is " manic " in type and is characterised by a sense of omnipotence, denial of psychic reality, and over-activity, all of which seek to deny the importance of the individual's good objects and to show contempt for them. The main aim of " manic defence " is to master and control all objects.

To sum up : The typical depressive phantasy might be crudely verbalised as follows—the good object is in pieces and cannot be put together again. In this connection although the child's relation to the father *imago* is referred to (particularly in connection with sadistic parents, and restitution phantasies concerning both parents), study of

---

* I.J.P.-A., 1935, vol. XVII, p. 174. Also a paper, "Mourning and its relation to Manic-depressive States," October 16th, 1938.

the clinical and theoretical contexts suggests that in so far as one object is referred to it is more often than not the mother *imago*. It is, however, specifically stated that " From the beginning the ego introjects objects " good " and " bad," for both of which its mother's breast is the prototype."

As has been noted, the publication of this paper marked the commencement of an entirely new orientation in psycho-analysis in a section of the British Society. The trend of discussions at subsequent meetings and the content of various papers soon indicated that a school of thought was developing based exclusively on a new hypothesis of development. Thus : in the following year Joan Riviere gave a paper[*] in which she suggested that the " manic defence " may motivate the " negative theraupeutic reaction." In this paper she accepted in their entirety Klein's ideas of the " depressive position " and of " manic defence." In a subsequent paper " On the genesis of psychical conflict in earliest infancy,"—which was expanded from an " exchange " lecture given at Vienna, she endeavoured to establish a systematic metapsychological basis for the new views. Clinically, the most significant point in this paper was contained in a footnote where she committed herself to the explicit statement : " *We have reason to think since Melanie Klein's latest work on depressive states that all neuroses are different varieties of defence against this fundamental anxiety, each embodying mechanisms which become increasingly available to the organism as its development proceeds.*" Readers who followed the history of Rank's deviation from psycho-analysis will not fail to note that by this time the Klein Group had also committed itself to a monistic theory of neurosogenesis. The validity of Klein's views was also accepted without reservation by several other members, e.g., in papers given to the Society by Drs. Winnicott, Rickman, Scott, Mrs. Isaacs, and Mrs. Rosenfeld[†] and in various contributions to discussions by Drs. Heimann and Matthew. In fact it was clear that the new views were going to be accepted by her adherents in the same spirit of unquestioning allegiance they had exhibited on the publication of Klein's first formulations. The situation in the British Society had, however, changed radically. A healthier tone of criticism was heard in its discussions. These criticisms were expressed on the first occasion[§] on which the Klein's new paper was discussed, and continued more or less unabated until an open split in the Society developed. For the most part they were advanced by myself and by Melitta Schmideberg. My main objections were as follows : (a) that the building-up of an " internalised-object-psychology " leads to confusion and obstruction instead of advancing existing concepts of early mental structure and function, e.g., confusion between " internalised-objects " and id-instincts, between " projection " and " expulsion," between an " objecto-imago," an "introjection," and a "body-phantasy";[¶] (b) that the " manic-defence " and " depressive position " are neither

---

[*] "A Contribution to the Analysis of the Negative Therapeutic Reaction," I.J.P.-A., 1936, vol. XVI, p. 304. I.J.P.-A., 1936, vol. XVII, p. 395.
[†] D. W. Winnicott, " Manic Defence,' December 4th, 1935. J. Rickman, " A Study of Quaker Beliefs, June 3rd, 1935, and " The Nature of Ugliness," January 20th, 1937. W. C. M. Scott, " Psycho-analysis of a Manic-depressive Patient in an Institution," June 2nd, 1937. S. Isaacs, " An Acute Psychotic Anxiety occurring in a Boy of Four Years," February 2nd, 1938; " The Nature of the Evidence concerning Mental Life in the Earliest Years," April 6th, 1938; " Temper-Tantrums in Early Childhood in their relation to Internal Objects," December 7th, 1938. E. Rosenfeld, " Psycho-analytic Approach in a Case of Psychosis," May 4th, 1938.
[§] October 6th, 1935.
[¶] In his paper on Introjection (I.J.P.-A., 1937, vol. XVIII, p. 269), Foulkes endeavoured to clear up the confusion arising out of various uses of this term.

clinical syndromes nor defence mechanisms, but a compound of already-established Freudian views with some inadequately substantiated theories; (c) and that although the existence of depressive reactions, both symptomatic, and in the case of the child, developmental, is beyond dispute, there is no justification for postulating a " central position " of this sort; (d) that although the relations of clinical depression to clinical mania are also indisputable, it does not follow that there is a central and genetic sequence; that manic defence is an arbitrarily constructed concept including such mechanisms as denial (Freud and Abraham) which really belong to different phases or aspects of ego-development (c.f. repression mechanisms); (e) that the " restitution " and " reparation " mechanisms associated with the " depressive position " are not organised until an obsessional phase that is clinically much later than that of depressive reactions; that some of the " mechanisms " described are not defence-mechanisms but phantasies, e.g., danger of injuring the object in the act of introjection; (f) that it has not yet been substantiated that analysts get better therapeutic results by basing their interpretations on the Klein hypotheses.

At the same time, and on many subsequent occasions, Melitta Schmideberg advanced similar criticisms, mainly: (a) that Melanie Klein's description of fixed sequences of psychotic positions is based on three assumptions, viz., the predominance of aggressive impulses, the predominance of projection and introjection mechanisms and the lack of reality sense in the infant. These assumptions have not, in M. Schmidebergs' view, been adequately substantiated, and in any case the new theory involves a neglect of the importance of libido, of the effect of environmental factors in earliest infancy and of mechanisms like repression, isolation, conversion, sublimation, etc., which to some extent counteract projection and introjection; (b) that one should distinguish between the frequency of clinical depression and the supposed theoretical importance of the "depressive position"; (c) that a developmental etiology that leaves hysteria out of account and neglects schizophrenia cannot be regarded as satisfactory; (d) that dynamic aspects of psychic situations are neglected; (e) that some of the phantasies described are not primitive but of later origin, and in any case are frequently *distortions* of reality reactions and of more objective anxieties; (f) that it is not satisfactory to explain clinical disturbances, e.g., paranoia, by displacing the symptom backwards into childhood, and that there is no proof that the processes described actually take place in babyhood; (g) that interpretations on the Klein model, by their very inexactitude, can act as reassurances, covering more preconscious worries and anxieties, by deflecting affect and criticism and encouraging flight into unreality.

In all these discussions the issue of environment factors in neurosogenesis entered. One of the main criticisms directed against the Klein system was its neglect of reality, to which it was replied that this lack of emphasis was more apparent than real. It was maintained by supporters of the method that not only did they study the interplay of environmental and endopsychic factors, but that the only way of understanding the importance of reality factors is to see them as refracted through the child's early anxiety situations and phantasies. In other words reality factors, whether occurring in childhood, in the current life-situation of the adult or in the transference, should not be assessed at face value but in terms of their " meaning " for the patient, which meaning is *a priori* an unconscious interpretation held to be made by the patient. To this line of argument M. Schmideberg replied (a) that the assumption of rigid sequences of positions cannot make proper allowance for environmental factors, in other words, environmental factors are regarded as merely of quantitative not of qualitative importance; (b) that reality factors are assessed in a tendentious way, that in particular there is displayed a bias in favour of the parents; the parents' self-valuation is accepted at face value; every event is interpreted on the assumption that the patient is guilty about it, and this gradually induces guilt in the patient; (c) that the neglect of reality factors and the stress laid on the " good mother " implies an idealisation of the mother-child relation and neglect of the ambivalence of both mother and child in more real levels.

The same author in a paper entitled " The Assessment of Environmental Factors " (February, 1936) stressed (a) the genetic importance of more continuous factors (in contrast to "traumatic" ones), operating even in the average or favourable environment; (b) the role of specific environmental factors in the first months of life; (c) the emotional attitude of the attendants, so often in contrast to their professed " modern " ideas; (d) that events repeatedly affecting derivatives of primitive instincts may exercise as marked an influence as those affecting the primary instincts themselves. She insisted that environmental factors should not be regarded in isolation, but always in the interplay of unconscious factors and mechanisms.

In these discussions questions of evidence and of verification of hypotheses inevitably arose. These focussed mainly on the assumptions made concerning mental processes in babyhood. These were considered in a series of " exchange " lectures between the British Society and the Vienna Society. Actually the exchange of views arose out of earlier differences concerning infantile development, but in practice it was limited to a discussion of the new hypotheses. In a paper given before the British Society,[*] R. Waelder challenged the views of Klein and Riviere. This constituted the Vienna reply to Riviere's paper on " The Genesis of Psychic Conflict in Earliest Infancy." Partly in reply to Waelder's criticism Susan Isaacs gave a paper on " The Nature of Evidence Concerning Mental Life in the Earliest Years " (April 6, 1938), concluding (from behaviouristic observations on babies and young children as well as from the analysis of older patients and children as young as $2\frac{1}{2}$ years) that preverbal phantasies already existed in the first months of life. She stressed the view that sometimes actual early experiences could be inferred in the course of later analysis, and supported the main argument in favour of drawing conclusions about babies from observations of older children by insisting on the principle of continuity. She also insisted that negative evidence should not be accepted as proof.

In the discussion M. Schmideberg objected to Isaacs' claims that negative evidence should be disallowed, and that there is no need to distinguish between analytic and behaviouristic observations. She maintained that Isaacs did not distinguish sufficiently between observations and the conclusions drawn from them; and demanded that the principle of continuity should be supplemented by that of development, adding that, as we are not likely ever to have absolute certainty on what goes on in the mind of a baby under six months, we should avoid

---
[*] The Problem of the Genesis of Psychical Conflict in Earliest Infancy," I.J.P.-A., vol. XVIII, p. 406.

dogmatism.*

As will be gathered from the above account it was inevitable that these differences should soon come to a head. That some delay occurred was due in part to the fact that between 1934 and 1938 the Freudian position in the Society was strengthened by the inclusion in the British Group of a number of colleagues from Austria and Germany, This accession of strength was also reflected in the Constitution of the Committee responsible for the training of candidates. The first signs of an open breach occurred in the summer of 1939 when as the result of differences in training the Training Committee began to consider whether it would not be advisable for Kleinian and Freudian candidates to be trained separately. The outbreak of war shelved the problem for a time, but after the Blitz and following prolonged discussion of the position the British Society decided to hold a "Controversial Series of Discussions" with the object of ascertaining whether Kleinian theories did or did not constitute a deviation from accepted Freudian teaching. The main effect of this decision was to stimulate the Klein Group to produce a formal Kleinian metapsychology. Hence although the issues under debate belong to what I have called the first and second phases of Kleinian theory, the metapsychological formulations deserve to be treated in a separate section.

* In the above summary I have drawn freely from the Appendix to " An Investigation of the Technique of Psycho-Analysis " by Glover and Brierley, 1940, Bailliere, Tindall and Cox.

IV
THE NEW KLEINIAN METAPSYCHOLOGY—1933-44

It may be said at once that even if the tendencies of Kleinian metapsychology had not already manifested themselves, it would not have been difficult to anticipate the lines they would follow. If you believe that infants after a few months of life develop phantasies of internal objects which predicate the existence of a super-ego, if further you believe that those phantasies are of such vital importances that they exert an uninterrupted influence on progressive mental development, and that they determine the formation of a "central depressive position;" finally if you believe that every variety of mental disorder can be traced back to this central position, you have certainly committed yourself to a quite novel metapsychology. You must prove that from the first all instinctual derivatives are what Freud would have called strongly cathected unconscious phantasy; further you must show that the mental apparatus possesses shortly after birth mechanisms that will preserve these apparently all powerful dynamic phantasies in a state of active cathexis throughout life, in other words, you must prove that the original Freudian unconscious system has at its core a central system or enclave as distinct from the rest of the unconscious as the Freudian unconscious is distinct from the Freudian pre-conscious; finally you must show that the continued existence of this enclave is the primary factor in all pathogenesis. The first of these steps was boldly undertaken by the Klein Group.*

(a) *The Kleinian Concept of Phantasy.* In her paper " The Nature and Function of Phantasy"† Susan Isaacs took up the following position :—Admitting that the Kleinian definition of phantasy extended the connotation of the term as used by Freud, Isaacs stated categorically " The primary content of all mental processes are unconscious phantasies." " Such phantasies are the basis of all unconscious and conscious thought processes." All words stand for concepts but "——the mind and mental process, thinking itself are not in themselves abstract. As experience, as we experience them, they are immediate." "Now in the infant experience and mental process must be primarily, perhaps at first entirely, affective, sensorial." " At the first level of experience introjection *is felt to be incorporation.* At a later level it is imagined to be incorporation later still it is felt to be getting something into the mind—that is to say into the ego, that part of the self as experienced which remembers and imagines and has emotions." Hence : " When the child feels he has dismembered his mother, his mental life is split and disintegrated." " The child experiences it as ' my mother-inside-me-is-in-bits'." "Phantasy is the mental corollary, the psychic representative of instinct, and there is no impulse, no instinctual urge which is not experienced as (unconscious) phantasy." Moreover : " Phantasy expresses the specific content of the urge (or the feeling, e.g., anxiety, fear, love and sorrow) which is dominating the child's mind at the moment, e.g., when he feels desires towards his mother, he experiences these as "I want to suck the nipple, to stroke her face, to eat her up,

---
* As this was an organised series of controversial discussions, it may be taken that the views expressed by the Kleinian representatives were fully endorsed by Melanie Klein herself. This was in fact the first occasion on which the views of her followers were officially subject to this disciplinary understanding
† Isaacs: Controversial Series I, also Discussion. January 27th, February 17th, May 19th, 1943.

to keep her within me, to bite the breast, to tear her to bits, to drown and burn her, to throw her out of me' and so on and so forth." And not only feels : "I want to : but : *I am doing* this." "The capacity to hallucinate," in Susan Isaac's opinion, "is either identical with phantasy or the precondition for it." The infant hallucinates "first, the nipple, then the breast, and later, his mother, the whole person" . . . "hallucination does not stop at the mere picture but carries him on to what he is, in detail, going to do with the desired object which he imagines (phantasies) he has obtained." " Thus we must assume that the introjection of the breast is bound up with the earliest forms òf phantasy life." Here Isaacs quotes from Riviere* a slightly different version of the situation. ". . . from the very beginning of life—the psyche responds to the reality of its experiences by interpreting them—or rather; by *mis*interpreting them—in a subjective manner that increases its pleasure and preserves it from pain." Here Riviere forcibly links this "act of a subjective interpretation of experience " with Freud's use of the term " hallucination." " This act . . . which is carried out *by means of* (my italics) the processes of introjection and projection, *is called by Freud hallucination* (my italics). Subsequently Isaacs expands her definition still further :— "Phantasies are in their simplest beginnings the content of *implicit meaning*, meaning latent in impulse, affect and sensation." This is repeated later in a confusing form. "As we have seen the earliest rudimentary phantasy is bound up with sensory experience ; it is an affective interpretation of bodily sensations, an expression of libibinal and aggressive impulses, operating under the pleasure-pain principle. Later on phantasy is inherent in sights and sounds, in touch and manipulation and perception of objects, as well as in gestures and vocal expression. At this stage it is still *implicit* phantasy."

After this statement of the Kleinian concept of phantasy, Isaacs commits herself and the Klein Group to the following fateful pronouncement, one which she openly agrees to be a deviation from the Freudian viewpoint : *"In the view I am here presenting, an essential feature of early mental development is the activity and intensity of early unconscious phantasies and their far-reaching and uninterrupted influence upon further progressive mental development."* (My italics.)

Finally on the nature of the evidence for these views, one of Isaac's statements deserves to be singled out : "When analytic experience leads us to reconstruct an internal situation or a particular relation to external reality, in the infant and young child, the behaviouristic data can say whether or not such a reconstruction is possible or likely, at the given age."

It remains to add that in the course of the prolonged discussion of her paper, Isaacs made one more significant statement regarding the nature of phantasy. She affirmed that " 'inner psychical reality' includes affects as well as phantasies but is otherwise indistinguishable."

The foregoing abstract of the Isaacs (Klein) position cannot convey fully the confusion to which the author (s) have reduced Freud's basic psychological concepts : this was more clearly brought out in the sections of the paper in which Isaacs strove laboriously to show by quotation from Freud's writings either that Freud himself would have favoured Kleinian conclusions or that these conclusions were merely natural extensions of Freudian concepts. Concerning these attempts the com-

---

* The Genesis of Psychic Conflict in Earliest Infancy. I.J.P.-A., 1936, vol. XVII, p. 399.

ment of A. Freud* sums up the situation effectively, viz., "To me it seems one of the most bewildering points about these new theories that existing analytic conceptions are explicitly retained and at the same time implicitly denied by the new formulations." To this I would add that Isaacs evidently found herself constantly *hampered* by existing Freudian concepts and that for the purposes of her own presentation she would have been well-advised to jettison them altogether and build up a separate psychological system with postulates of her own.† To clarify the situation I have drawn up a list of the Freudian concepts, positions and definitions that are either confused, weakened or set aside by the Kleinian system. In the first place Freud's distinctions between a memory-trace, an image, a "thing-presentation," an object-imago, a phantasy, an introjection and an identification are lost. They are all at one time or another subsumed under the Kleinian term "phantasy." Similarly the distinction between hallucinatory regression of instinct excitation to the sensory end of the psychic apparatus, a hallucinatory phantasy (clinically, hallucination) and phantasy (whether unconscious or preconscious) is lost. The concept of instinct derivatives is confused and in effect the fundamental distinction of affect from ideational presentation is lost. Distinctions between positive (tension or discharge) affects and reactive affects, in the long run, between gratification and frustration, are blurred; consequently the distinction between reality-ego-systems and phantasy-systems disappears. The relations between psychical reality, reality-proving and phantasy (in the Freudian sense) are obliterated. And both theoretically and practically (e.g., in Isaacs' description of Kleinian stages of phantasy) the distinction between the unconscious, the pre-conscious and the conscious is blurred. Not only so the distinction between the Id and the Ego is flattened out. For although Freud agreed that the boundaries are hard to delimit, yet it is obvious that in her concept of "implicit meaning" and of its (somewhat contradictory) congener, "implicit phantasy," Isaacs is simply telling us what she (Isaacs) thinks the Primitive Ego would think if it (the Primitive Ego) could think and knew what was going on in the Id. In other words, what the Freudian would call Id-activity, the Kleinian calls implicit Ego (or Super-ego) phantasy.§

It would require several papers to trace all of these deviations from Freudian psychology to their roots, for although on occasion the deviation is directly stated or easily inferred, on others one has to follow the concept through a maze of exposition and definition watching carefully the exact meaning of the words employed. To give some examples: referring to the use by A. Freud of the phrase "the mother-image in the child's mind." Isaacs says "Now I feel that this description of the 'mother-image in the child's mind' comes very close to Klein's postulate that the child introjects his mother"; and again "Anna Freud (to my mind) *implies* phantasies when she speaks of the 'mother-image in the child's mind'." Here the deviation is obvious enough. On the question of instinct derivatives, i.e., affect and mental presentations (a distinction of supreme importance to the

---
* Discussion, January 27th, 1943.
† I have expressed this conviction in the title I have given to this paper.
§ A good example of the importation of the observer's opinions into alleged unconscious phantasies was afforded by Isaacs during the discussion. A. Freud criticised a statement by Isaacs, viz., "the infant identifies the mother who does *not* remove a pain with the pain itself." This, A. Freud held, proved that in Isaacs' opinion negation existed in the unconscious. In reply Isaacs said, "I would agree that my way of stating this fact was open to her interpretation, although I did not intend it. I was condensing in this statement the observer's !nowledge and the infant's experience."

dynamics of mind), the reader may best appreciate the confusion Isaacs introduces by perusing the following summary of her views on the subject, viz :—unconscious phantasies are the primary content of all mental processes; in the infant experience and mental process must be primarily, perhaps at first entirely affective, sensorial: the child experiences his psychic reality in terms of his phantasy life; the "mental expression of instinctual needs," (a phrase used by Freud), "*is*," says Isaacs, "unconscious phantasy," phantasy is the mental corollary, the psychic representative of instinct; phantasy expresses the specific content of the urge (*or the feeling*), anxiety, fear, love or sorrow; (yet), it soon becomes a means of defence *against* (my italics) anxieties; phantasies are in their simplest beginnings implicit meaning, meaning latent in impulse, affect and sensation; (and finally) inner psychical reality includes affects as well as phantasies but is otherwise indistinguishable (from phantasy). Yet when Foulkes* taxed her with regarding phantasies as "primary motors," the reply given on behalf of the Klein Group by Heimann† was "unconscious phantasy is the mental representative of instinct: the conclusion being that unconscious phantasy is charged with instinctual energy," indicating thereby either that the Klein Group has forgotten about affect-energy or that they believe affect-energy has no dynamic effect or that it is identical with the cathexis of a mental presentation!

During the discussion many other arguments were led against the new Kleinian definition. A. Freud,§ for example, pointed out that the new definition not only extended the reference of the term to include a number of early mental processes under a common connotation, but also "narrows it down from use for conscious as well as unconscious processes to use for the unconscious only"; adding that no regard was paid to whether the mental processes are instinct-derivatives or not. Moreover she held that although Isaacs described unconscious phantasies as being partly subject to the primary process, she implicitly rejected the action of other important factors in the primary process. In A. Freud's view unconscious life, as described by Isaacs, included important characteristics of the secondary process. To which Isaacs replied, "the *Ucs* does include different sorts of processes and must not be taken to refer only to the earliest most primitive aspects of the mind, the primary processes." To this A. Freud countered that while a correlating function applied to perception and reality testing from birth onwards, this synthetic function is not applied during the first year of instinctual urges. She might well have asked why, if the secondary process applied also to primary unconscious phantasy, there was such an overpowering need to emphasise unconscious phantasy as the (apparently sole) expression of instinct and mental life. If anything emerges from the study of early Kleinian phantasies and of their exposition it is that the phantasies themselves combine characteristics of unconscious, preconscious and conscious mental systems, to say nothing of possible contributions from the mental systems of their discoverers.

But when all is said, the most effective way of uncovering the poverty of the Isaacs (Klein) postulates is to outline again Freud's orderly series of concepts regarding the mental apparatus, concepts which we are invited to barter for the hypothetical benefits of hypothetical Klein-

---
* Discussion. February 7th, 1943.
† Discussion. March 17th, 1943.
§ Discussion. January 27th, 1943.

ian "phantasies." Starting with the concept of a central mental apparatus dealing with instinctual excitation, governing the approaches to motility, and having a sensory receiver, Freud went on to describe the organisation of memory traces in the various ψ systems. These traces which form the groundwork of ego organisation record a pleasure-pain series of experiences. And since, in contrast to the isolated stimulations of the external world, the stimulations of instinct are continuous, the earliest memory-trace systems are concerned primarily with various degrees of gratification or frustration of impulse. But since the ultimate aim of all instincts is gratification, the most important trace systems (which when cathected by psychic energy constitute memory images) are those which extend the "aim."[*] These images have as it were been burned into the mind through their respective association with psychic pain or pleasure. The realisation of the aim thus comes to be the primary concern of the psychic apparatus. The pleasure principle is bound up with this dynamic aim. The function of memory together with memory images is however an adaptation function first and mainly developed in response to frustration. But so long as (what ultimately proves to be) the object of the instinct promotes the gratification of (what proves to be) the subject's aim (as in the case of the most important, infantile needs) this function remains larval. Nevertheless it is a potential reality function, which after pleasure-pain experiences have led to the distinction of the self from the not-self develops into a reality proving ego-function. In other words, when frustration becomes acute the cathecting of pleasure and pain image-associations develops reality value. The cathexis of images promoting activities that accelerate gratification and of images leading to avoidance of activities that increase frustration, adds to the probability that instinct tension will be reduced. Summation of experiences of reduced tension leads ultimately to the development of reality proving and this in turn promotes correlation between the subject, aim and the object of any given instinct. Not until this stage has been reached can we talk of object formation. Although therefore it is true that the pleasure principle dominates psychic life in the early stages, the pleasure-pain series of experience puts a premium on the development of reality proving. In this sense the baby, once the larval stages are passed, has, relative to its conditions of life, just as good a sense of reality-proving for any given instinct aim as any grown-up. The fact that the mind is dominated by the pleasure principle does not mean that the pleasure principle is invariably successful. At this stage therefore, there is no question of describing the cathexis of memory-trace-systems as "meaning." Indeed even if an observer were asked to describe what *he* thought about the baby's state of mind, he would have no need to say more than that the baby, despite alternating states of experience of pleasure (gratification) and pain (frustration), on the whole pursued the main *aim* of all instincts, viz., gratification. But that would of course be the observer's interpretation, not the baby's "phantasy."

To the consideration of these "progressive" (developmental and adaptation) aspects of mental activity Freud added some important formulations regarding the "regressive" tendencies of the mental apparatus. The relation of these regressive tendencies to pre-natal

[*] See also A. Freud "What I mean to imply in my description of the Child's narcissistic state, is a stage in which the aim of the instinct is of overwhelming importance, whereas the object is only dimly taken into account." Discussion. April 7th, 1943.

life has not been fully established,* but of the post-natal factors one of the most important is the peculiar nature of frustrations existing during sleep, a state which occupies by far the larger part of the daily life of infants. This regressive tendency of the mental apparatus must of course be distinguished clinically from the regression mechanisms occurring, for example, prior to symptom formation. It is characterised by a backward flow of frustrated instinctual energy from the motor to the sensory end of the psychic apparatus. The qualitative aspects of this instinct tension have not been fully examined but we may be sure that a certain amount of summation of different instinct charges occurs, giving rise quantitatively to an acute damming-up of energy. Anyhow, the result is what is described as an attempt at hallucinatory gratification. The psychic relief secured (or sampled) in this attempt varies in accordance with the depth of sleep and the intensity of frustration but when previous pleasure experiences have been intense or when previous frustrations have been acute, the hallucinatory process is no doubt compensatory as well as being an unsuccessful attempt at adaptation. And it is of some relevance to the discussion of early reality processes that this compensatory pleasure is heightened when the hallucinatory regression frees energy once more in the direction of motility, and some *actions appropriate to the hallucinatory activation of images occur*—as in sucking movements during sleep. But this is possibly only a marginal increase. *The part release of appropriate motility is in itself a proof of the reality nature of the images cathected in the regression to the sensory end of the apparatus.* The hallucinatory process is an attempt at gratification initiated by frustration, but arrested at the imaginal level and so doomed to failure.

Now there is nothing here to justify the Kleinian equation of memory-images, unconscious phantasies, introjections and " internal objects." There is no question of using the term " phantasy " for such psychic events. There is an essential distinction between on the one hand image presentations, whether associated with reality gratification or with the attempts at hallucinatory gratification (i.e., regression to the sensory end) and on the other hand any variety of phantasy either conscious or unconscious. Phantasy in the sense in which it is used by Freud is a much later, more complicated and from the point of view of reality a more revolutionary development. Possibly the confusion arose in the Klein system because of slipshod thinking regarding the clinical hallucinations observed in the psychoses. The fact that a schizophrenic may behave as if his phantasies are real is no proof of the existence of these phantasies in the first months of life.† The ruling psychic concept is not " phantasy," it is the concept of " imaginal presentations " (based on the organisation of memory traces) and of their cathexis. Development in the direction of reality thinking and of phantasy can then be traced in an orderly series and correlations made that are appropriate to their respective exciting causes. Not only is the behaviouristic study of sucklings in favour of Freud's system, but the whole weight of biological evidence of survival is against the Kleinian assumption. As I have pointed out, when the infant's hallucinations of sucking obtain some expression in motility, the actions are appropriate not to a Kleinian phantasy but to the reality of sucking. It is a sound assumption therefore that during this sensorial regression the instinct has retained a realistic aim. In this respect the infant is neither a fool nor a phantast.

* See also H. Hoffer. Discussion. April 17th, 1943.
† See also Schmideberg, *op. cit.* and Foulkes, *op. cit.*

Moreover, if Isaac's view that reality thinking is a derivative of primary phantasy thinking were correct, our existing conception of the function, timing and psychic locality of unconscious defence mechanisms would have to be completely re-cast. It would imply, for example, that ego-syntonic as well as ego-dystonic presentations are subject to repression and that in some way or another, ego-syntonic impulses contrive to escape this censorship. It is to my mind unthinkable that presentations of instinct, in particular those advancing the aim of preservation, which are capable of conscious gratification without interference from unconscious defence-mechanisms (bewusstseinsfaehig) should begin to be distinguished at some later date from an original phantasy nexus. Again the whole weight of biological evidence of survival is against the assumption. *By abolishing the distinction between cathected memory-traces and phantasies Isaacs abolishes the economic function of repression and thereby obliterates the distinction between the dynamic unconscious and the preconscious.*

To sum up: The history of reality thinking and phantasy thinking is a long and complicated one. The former can be traced back from its final conceptual form through the processes of "word presentations" and "thing presentations" to the earliest formation of memory traces. Its development is influenced by the pleasure-pain series, the operation of reality proving and the expansion of the reality principle. On the other hand the beginnings of phantasy are determined by three factors; the failure of the halllucinatory process, the development of object formation, and the action of repression. The existence of phantasy implies the psychic capacity to form correlations between the subject, aim and object of an instinct. Purely narcissistic organisation comes to an end wih the failure of the hallucinatory technique. Phantasy in the Freudian sense is a frustration product which should be set off not so much against reality-thinking as against reality-action. Without the mechanism of repression, effective unconscious cathexis of phantasy could not be maintained. Despite all the involved discussion of instinct derivatives and of the relation between " psychic reality " and so-called " external reality " there is no difficulty in either the statement or the comprehension of these ideas that has not already been met in Freud's basic formulations. On the barest grounds, therefore, of economy of hypothesis, there is no justification for the Kleinian theory of phantasy.

But it is high time to return to the list of Kleinian deviations from Freudian theory. To continue: the biological progression of an instinct-series (the Freudian development of the libido) with its psychological implications of fixation points and of a regression series is sacrificed for the sake of the Kleinian oro-phallic ego* and/or super-ego of the first year which constitutes according to her an independent, dynamic and (except presumably to Kleinian therapeutists) immutable system. Friedlander† summed up the situation as follows :—
" We see that the Freudian conception of regression is of course intimately bound up with Freud's conception of libidinal development up to the genital phase. This conception is based on the biological tendency of the instincts to develop. Contrariwise in Mrs. Klein's view . . . . The so-called early phantasies which we can only perceive as being

---
* I have coined the term in order to emphasise one of the descriptive features of the Klein system. It is worth noting that although Klein talks of the factors of anal and urethral erotism, she neglects the all-important factors of e.g., gastro-intestinal and skin erotism in ego differentiation.
† Discussion. January 27th, 1943.

inborn or universally formed in the first months of life and which already contain oral, anal-sadistic and phallic impulses as well as guilt-feelings and defence mechanisms, are thought to be of primary importance in so far as the further development occurs as a flight from too great a fear or too great a guilt-feeling aroused by these phantasies " . . " Naturally, therefore, the conception of regression has no place in this theory. The whole of the libido remains fixated to these early phantasies throughout life. . . . The important fact which emerges from these ideas is not, in my opinion, that Mrs. Klein lays less stress on a mechanism on which Freudian lay more stress. The importance of the depreciation of the mechanism of regression, which Mrs. Isaacs admits as such, is the fact that it is the result of givng up Freud's conception of the biological development of the libido."

Following this line of thought it is possible to outline clearly one of the clinical bones of contention between the Kleinian and the Freudian Groups, viz., the importance of the classical Oedipus situation. Freudians hold that the Klein Group depreciate the importance of the classical Oedipus situation, both clinically and theoretically. To which the Kleinians reply that they do not—that on the contrary they emphasise how important it is by discovering the Oedipus complex in the sixth month of life. But their assumption of a primary active core in the *ucs* based on the persisting cathexis of unconscious phantasies at this period —a core which, according to Isaacs, retains its power to influence all later progressive mental development, commits them to a depreciation of the specific significance of the classical Oedipus situation. Her views of the dynamic significance of " early phantasy " and her views on regression may still allow her to plead that the classical Oedipus phase has a secondary significance. Yes, but a significance shorn of dynamic importance. Freud's view was that whatever the pregenital phases of infancy contribute, the Oedipus phase, as described by him, is of primary significance in the dynamic, economic and structural aspects of the term.

Indeed we may conveniently close the provisional list of deviations by considering the economic and topographic implications of the Kleinian theory of phantasy. These turn on the relation of the pleasure-principle to stages of auto-erotism and narcissism, and to the beginnings of object relationship. This issue was stated succinctly by A. Freud* as follows:—" One of the outstanding differences between Freudian and Kleinian theory is that Mrs. Klein sees in the months of life evidence of a wide range of differentiated object-relations, partly libidinal and partly aggressive. Freudian theory on the other hand allows at this period only for the crudest rudiments of object-relationship and sees life governed by the desire for instinct gratification in which perception of the object is only slowly achieved." Again " The assumption of early object-phantasies in Mrs. Klein's theories is bound up with the theoretical substitution of a very early stage of life and varied object-relationship, for the early phases of narcissism and auto-erotism as described by Freud." And again " I consider that there is a narcissistic and autoerotic phase of several months duration which precedes what we call object relationship in its proper sense, even though the beginnings of object-relaxation are slowly built up during this initial stage. According to Mrs. Isaacs' descriptions, the newborn infant, already in the first six months loves, hates, desires, attacks, wishes to destroy and to dismember his mother." " According to my own

---
* Discussion. April 7th, 1943.

conception of this same period, the infant is at this time exclusively concerned with his own well-being." " I believe that the psychic processes (during the child's narcissistic state) are governed by the urge for satisfaction, that is by the aim of the instinct and not by phantasies of its object." "It is . . . in agreement with the Freudian conception of a narcissistic beginning of life to conceive of auto-erotism as an intrinsic source of pleasure, independent of relations to the object." Lantos* put the position in the following way. Referring to the primitive reactions, actions and play of the child, she wrote : " We believe that bodily functions, the functioning of the sensory apparatus are pleasurable in themselves. So is mental development wth its gradual acquisition of knowledge and understanding." . . . " they are all the same in so far as they are pleasures in themselves, that is to say : pleasures without meaning." " Thumb-sucking, masturbation, hair pulling and other habits are at that age still autoerotic." " We do not believe that masturbation makes him (the infant) feel : ' I shall bring my mother back.' " " The difference (between Freudian and Kleinian views) is not that we are building on different facts (behaviouristic observations) but that we are interpreting the same facts differently."

In the introductory part of this paper I pointed out that for some time a gap existed between psycho-analytic formulations concerning mental life at the latest pre-Oedipus stage and hypothetical reconstructions of the primitive ego : also that the tendency of most analysts then was to regard developments occurring prior to the immediately pre-Oedipus stage as belonging to the primitive phase. On various occasions I maintained that the application of the terms auto-erotism and narcissism to these comparatively advanced stages was no longer justified. In this respect I held that the terms had "to some extent outworn their usefulness." In particular I found the concept of a unified stage of late narcissism an obstacle to understanding, and when I developed the " nuclear theory of ego-formation " I became convinced that only in the earliest stages of infantile development could either term be used with advantage and then only provided one kept in mind the scattered forms of early ego-organisation. But this issue is not at present in dispute. Existing controversies, as A. Freud pointed out, turn on the Kleinian definition of the term phantasy, the date of phantasy and the content of Kleinian phantasy. And so we come back once more to the dispute over " meaning " or " implicit meaning." I would only add a few considerations appropriate to the discussion of auto-erotism and narcissism in the first year of life. In the first place the concept of auto-erotism is bound up with the polymorphous nature of infantile sexuality.† It takes cognisance of the fact that whereas certain components of sexuality are (whether the infant knows it or not) anaclitic in nature in the sense that their complete gratification requires the support and collusion of (what the observer knows to be) an external object, other components are comparatively independent of external objects. Some of the most important erotisms, e.g., skin and muscle erotism, are of this nature. And it is precisely the autonomic function of many of the early erotisms that promotes a narcissistic organisation of the early ego (in my view, early ego-nuclei). In the early stages even those libidinal gratifications that involve the collusion of (what the observer knows to be) an external object are, *qua* experiences, of an "auto-erotic" char-

---
* Discussion. January 27th, 1943.
† The polymorphous structure of early ego-nuclei seems to me entirely congruous with concepts of "components" of sexuality.

acter. They can have an object reference only when (a) the object has been distinguished from the subject (b) the object imago has been cathected with instinctual energy. " Meaning " whether attached to reality presentations or later to phantasy presentations is a product of frustration which implies the capacity to correlate the affective derivatives of instinct with both subject and object. Without frustration there would be no more " meaning " in extra-uterine life than there is in intra-uterine life. After sleep, and reality gratification of hunger needs, auto-erotism affords the closest approximation to a frustration-free existence—although admittedly it involves expenditure of both physical and physical effort. Later no doubt auto-erotisms acquire meaning in both realistic and phantastic senses of the term but it is significant that autoerotic libidinal components that escape the processes of sublimation are by comparison with object impulses singularly ineducable. In short, however desirable it may be to extend our knowledge of early object relations there is no advantage to be gained by presuming, as Klein does, organised and unified ego patterns at a time when, according to the overwhelming weight of clinical evidence and of theoretical probability only a scattered and uncorrelated series of organisations of memory traces can be presumed.

(b) *Introjection and Projection.* The next stage in the development of Kleinian metapsychology consisted in applying to the description of mental *mechanisms* the Kleinian concepts described in the previous section, together with some of the assumptions laid down as axiomatic during the " first phase " of Kleinian theory. It is obvious for example, that if there is no difference between an image, an imago, a phantasy, a meaning, an introjection, an "internal object" and a super-ego that is capable of being "ejected" and if all this primary mental activity is thought of in terms of oral experience, it will not be long before mental mechanisms are equated with bodily processes. This is in fact what happened. Speaking officially on behalf of the Klein Group, Heimann[*] began with the following statement : " I shall use the terms introject and project when referring to the mental mechanisms which are modelled on and correspond to the bodily experiences of taking in and expelling respectively." (The baby) " devotes an intense attention to his surroundings (to the objects around him) . . . the modification of his mental apparatus through this function of attention and of his " tasting " the stimuli comes about by his *taking in* with his mouth *and hands and eyes and ears* (my italics) every object which attracts his attention ; his first attempts to make acquaintance with any new thing are expressed in efforts to take hold of it and suck or taste it. *As he does so he actually introjects it ;* in his experience he incorporates it, sucks it in, eats it up." " The *earliest relation* to an object is effected by means of introjecting it." " . . . the most fundamental vital processes of any living organism consist of intake and discharge. ". . the mechanism of taking in and expelling, or if we think of their psychical correlates introjecting and projecting, are vital processes of the first magnitude. "In the *ucs* the oral significance of growth and acquisition and the anal significance of loss and gift are maintained, so that under circumstances in which this fundamental pattern becomes reactivated all acquiring means devouring, all giving means spitting and defaecating *with the result* (my italics) that guilt and anxiety arise along with these

---

[*] " Some Aspects of the Role of Introjection and Projection in Early Development." Controversial Series II; also Discussions. October 20th, November 17th, 1943.

activities." "The earliest introjections establish a protective and a persecuting agency within the mind ("good" and "bad" breast). "The early introjections represent the early stages of the later genital super-ego." "The introjected breast is the object of the infant's auto-erotic wishes and experiences." .. " . . . the narcissistic condition is bound up with a libidinal cathexis of internal objects." ". . . we should not draw a sharp line between auto-erotism and narcissism." "Hallucinatory gratification may be considered as the supreme instance of auto-erotic activity." . . . (it) is based on the relation to a "good" inner breast, which the infant rediscovers in a part of his own body " . . (it) is stronger when its object is a part, i.e., the nipple, than when it is a whole person : for the nipple was really " inside " the infant, completely enclosed by the lips, the gum and the tongue " . . . "the first roots of the super-ego are to be found in the introjected "good" and "bad" breast, to which are added the "good" and "bad" parents and the " good " and " bad " penis."

As in the case of the summary of Isaacs' paper, this abstract of the more significant parts of Heimann's paper cannot convey the utter confusion of psychological thinking displayed by the author. One sample must suffice : having quoted passages from ' Beyond the Pleasure Principle' in which Freud, discussing the protective functions of *cell structure*, refers to the differentiated outer layer of the living vesicle whose protective function against outer stimuli is almost more important than its receptive function, Heimann goes on to say " what Freud describes in those and other passages is that the Ego, the surface part of the Id, comes into being and functions by means of both *taking things* (my italics) into itself and conversely rejecting them from itself." Now in fact Freud was not then considering " taking things " into the Ego, he was discussing the biological function of a protective layer (the concept of the Reizschutz) and he went on to point out that in more highly developed organisms, the *sense organs* constitute such a protective "layer." Freud never suggested as Heimann does that the mouth is a rudimentary thought organ taking precedence over the central nervous system. The fact is that Heimann, following Klein, converts analogies into literal identities. " Taking in things " and " rejecting " them are, as Heimann's later argument indicates, regarded as *identical* with introjection which (see Isaacs) is identical with the " experience," " psychic reality feeling " and " meaning " of actually taking the nipple into the mouth or spitting out of the mouth. But Heimann goes on. " Thus the *mechanism* of taking in* *recurs* in the operation of attention." Then comes a slight change. The function of keeping out dangerous *stimuli* "is akin to the function of discharge and expulsion," Apparently dissatisfied with the use of " akin," she adds, " However it *is*† an expulsion in so far as the *decision* not to *let in* the dangerous stimuli, presupposes that a small sample of it has been taken in, *decided upon* as being *bad*, and *expelled* and the *whole* from which the sample was *taken, kept out* in consequence of the *judgement* to which the sample was subjected."

Paragraphs of this kind, with which, to adopt an appropriate phrase, the paper is replete would justify any reviewer in dismissing any con-

---
* Note that this is now a mechanism.
† Only the word "is" is underlined in the original: the other italics in these passages are intended to draw the reader's attention to two facts (a) that even when elaborating a biological analogy Heimann falls into confusion between biological and psychical function; (b) that the resultant confused ideology is anthropomorphised and expressed in terms of consciousness.

clusions based on them. But it is a characteristic of Kleinian metapsychology that the conclusions do not follow from the argument: rather is the argument an *apologium* for the conclusions. The conclusions themselves are nothing more than postulates. Hence it is important to single out the main tendencies to which they give expression. For example, it is clear that *Kleinian views on introjection and projection merely paraphrase in pseudo-metapsychological terminology the phantasies alleged to exist in the oro-phallic phase described by Klein in her "Psycho-analysis of Children," phantasies which were never more than unsubstantiated assumptions.* But the tendency is much more significant than this fact would indicate. Brierley* remarked that to limit ourselves to understanding the subjective meaning of our unconscious pre-conceptions about mental processes and to equate these with the processes themselves would be comparable to limiting our knowledge of the outer world to perceptual knowledge. *She might as well have said quite frankly that this equation is the basis of mysticism.*

For the same reason it is instructive to read the passages in Heimann's paper where she seeks to fortify Kleinian theories by an appeal to the Freudian concept of the Death-instinct. Having discussed the concepts of Life-instincts and Death-instincts at some length, Heimann reaches a very remarkable conclusion. " Here " she says "we have to face the fact that the aims of the instincts to which the organism is subject are in opposition to one another; in other words that (my italics) *we deal with an organism which is by its very nature in a condition of conflict.*" Lest the use of the term " organism " should confuse the issue, the following quotations make clear that Heimann is thinking of *psychic* conflict :—" One conceives of the human mind as being by its very nature compelled to manipulate constantly between two fundamentally opposed instincts." " And since the instincts are inborn, we have to conclude that *some form of conflict exists from the beginning of life.*" Now it is hardly necessary to take this point seriously. As Friedlander† put it, "This misconception leads at once to a further psycho-analytical impossibility, namely to the fight of two instincts without intervention of what we call the mind." And again: " The further result of this misconception is the theory (advanced by Heimann) that the life-instinct employs a defence-mechanism, namely, projection, against the death-instinct. In Freudian theory defence mechanisms are employed by the Ego against the instincts." Indeed in her own reply Heimann§ herself provided the complete refutation of her own remarkable theory. She stated that she uses the term deathinstinct when discussing theoretical matters, but that when dealing with clinical considerations she uses the term " destructive instinct." But what else is the concept of " conflict " but a clinical concept? All this confused theorising is however less significant than the tendency it expresses. Foulkes¶ discussing the Isaacs-Klein concept of phantasy remarked : " It looks as if we were back at the religious and spiritual level with an independent soul having energies of its own from another world. This is particularly true when these phantasies have attained

---

* Discussion. October 20th, 1943.
† Discussion. October 20th, 1943.
§ Discussion. November 17th, 1943.
¶ Discussion. February 7th, 1943. The subject had already been considered exhaustively in a paper by M. Schmideberg " ' Introjected Objects ': an issue of Terminology or a Clinical problem?" (3, xii: 1941). See also her papers "Proof and Error in Psycho-analytic Conclusions " (6, xi 1940): " The Relative Validity of ' Preconscious ' and ' Deep ' Interpretations " (19, iii, 1941): " Projection, Introjection and Identification."

the dignity of ' inner objects.' " In Heimann's paper we can trace the outlines of a new religious biology. The ultimately moral values " good " and " bad " can be followed back to early phantasies of "good" and "bad" introjected breasts, and, via the function of taking in the good and expelling the bad, to a " conflict " between the Life and the Death-instincts which exists before any psychic organisation is developed. *Whatever else this may mean, it certainly represents a projection into biological science of moral values.*

Considerations of space forbid the follow-up of many other and equally phantastic theories comprising the Heimann (Klein) system, nevertheless, the correlations between auto-erotism, narcissism, introjection and "internal objects" are worthy of some scrutiny. The significant point here is not so much the confusion Heimann introduces into the Freudian definitions of auto-erotism and narcissism (after all no student of psycho-analysis will have much difficulty in distinguishing between a mode of instinct gratification and an organisation of the ego) as the implied efflorescence in the ego of " internal objects," which become the " object " of " auto-erotic " impulses. The logical conclusion of all this is not evaded either by Heimann or Klein. It is that hallucinatory gratification is based on the relation to a good " inner " (and presumably therefore introjected) breast which the infant discovers in a part of his body. Now a moment's consideration will show that if hallucinatory gratification is the supreme instance of auto-erotic activity (Heimann-Klein) and if the capacity to hallucinate is either identical with phantasy or the pre-condition of it (Isaacs-Klein) and further if phantasy is the psychic representative of instinct (Isaacs-Klein-Riviere), and still further if auto-erotism has an introjected object (Heimann-Klein), then presumably object-formation and introjection must exist before the hallucinatory process reaches its height, i.e., in the first months of life. Thus hallucination is at one time regarded as identical with phantasy or the pre-condition of it at another it is the " post-condition " of introjection. In other words, mental organisation exists before there is any mental organisation. Not only so, the " death-instinct " ideologies produced by the Klein school are by the same token put out of action; *according to their own definitions of hallucination and autoerotism only libidinal instincts can exist.*

Now all this is absurd enough, but it is not so important as the tendency of the thinking responsible for the confusion. Studying all these tendencies it is difficult to escape the conclusion that Klein and her adherents in their anxiety to establish the validity of Klein phantasies have been led into postulating a purely mystical conception of early mental life. As I pointed out earlier this is one of the dangers of undisciplined "reconstruction." *In my opinion the Klein system has broken through the limitations of metapsychology to postulate a bioreligious system which depends on faith rather than on science.*

(c) *The Concept of Regression.* In the first two papers of the Controversial Series, discussion was essentially non-clinical. But when it comes to a discussion of the concept of regression it is increasingly easy to confuse the meta-psychological with the clinical aspects of the subject, and consequently increasingly important to distinguish between them. No such distinction was effected by the Klein protagonists. In their joint paper on Regression, Heimann and Isaacs[*] continued to assume that Kleinian phantasy systems existing from the sixth month

---

[*] Controversial Series III, also Discussion. January, February, 1944.

of life were not in dispute, although in fact these phantasies were the original cause of the Controversy. Discussing the data regarding fixation the authors maintained that the relation of libidinal wishes to impulses of aggression " can be directly noted " : anxiety and the earliest defences against it " can be seen " : the child's relations to his objects together with his phantasies "can be studied" : early processes of symbol-formation, etc., " can be watched," and so forth. The casual reader might not realise that in fact there are no such direct notes, views, studies and observations. There are only *interpretations* of the infant's behaviour or utterances from which *hypothetical reconstructions* are arrived at. Nevertheless it is impossible to discuss regression without entering on the clinical field, and it is equally impossible to modify the Freud concept of regression without altering the Freudian theory of neurosogenesis*.

Starting with the relation of anxiety to fixation Heimann and Isaacs stated, " When stirred too intensely (by whatever situation) anxiety contributes to a fixation of the libido at that point. . . " A fixation is thus partly to be understood as a defence against anxiety." If, however, anxiety is not overpowering it " acts as a spur to libidinal development. " Anxiety itself, however . . . . arises from aggression." " It is the destructive impulses of the child in the oral and anal phases which are, through the anxiety they stir up, the prime causes of the fixation of the libido." Frustration initiates aggression " not only by a simple ' damming-up ' of the libido but also by evoking hate and aggression and consequent anxiety." This cannot be understood " without appreciating the part played by *phantasies* " . . . . " phantasies of the destruction of the desired object of devouring, expelling, poisoning, burning, etc., etc., with ensuing dread of total loss of the source of life and love, the " good " object, as well as the dread of retaliation, persecution and threat to the subject's own body from the destroyed and dangerous " bad " object." " The primal oral and anal anxieties give rise to the homosexual fixation and to the *regression to paranoia* (my italics)." Under non-traumatic conditions they can influence development favourably. Thus " These oral phantasies and aims have remained uninterruptedly active in the unconscious mind exerting a favourable influence and promoting genitality." " Bound up with these phantasies, moreover, are the reparative tendencies." " In our view the part played by internal objects and the super-ego is an essential part in the regressive process." Discussing Freud's theory of the Life and Death-instincts, the authors remark : " The question now arises whether regression is not the outcome of a failure of the libido to master the destructive impulses and anxiety aroused by frustration." Agreeing that Freud's view of inhibition was bound up with excessive erogenicity of the organ concerned, Heimann and Isaacs say " We venture to think that it is precisely this, the phantasy of violence, derived from the admixture of destructiveness which causes anxiety and guilt and enforces—by the intervention of the super-ego— an inhibition of that activity."

As will be seen from this summary the paper contains a good deal of the Kleinian theorising already described in my account of the " first phase." Thus, speaking of animal phobias the authors quote Klein's view that underlying it is " not only the fear of being castrated, but a still earlier fear of being *devoured by the super-ego* (my italics)." On

---

* See also W. Hoffer and Friedlander. Discussion. January, 1944.

occasion the most controversial formulations consist of conclusions, which in turn are drawn from conclusions based originally on interpretations. The promotion of genitality by the original introjection of a " good " breast is based on the theory of " uninterrupted activity " of oral phantasies "exerting" a favourable "influence." This in turn is based on the postulation of these early phantasies and introjections, and, as I have pointed out earlier, *implies the existence of a primary enclave in the Freudian ucs, an independent and permanently active core through which all instinct must always pass.*

Regarding the relation of the libido to destructiveness, the authors take the view that analysts in the past put too exclusive emphasis on the role of the libido in regression because the libido was the first instinct energy to be studied. Whereas the truth is that libidinal regression was emphasised because of the *nature* of the libido. It is a commonplace that despite their adhesiveness, libidinal impulses are by comparison with other instincts remarkably labile. It is this lability which, together with the prolonged history of modification of different phases of sexuality, prepares the way for subsequent regression ; in other words the reversal of this process is the main feature of regression. The sexual impulses can change their aims as well as their objects. Aggressive impulses may change objects but modify their aims to a comparatively small degree. It is true that certain varieties of "fused" impulse appear to behave as if the sadistic component had a specific aim, but it should not be forgotten that the libido acts as the pilot impulse both in the fusion and in the sadism. Both biologically and psychologically regarded, it is in the highest degree improbable that regression operates primarily through the aggressive series. This is supported by the constant reactive function preserved by aggressive impulses. If aggressive impulses possessed the same lability of aim as the libidinal impulses, not only would their general biological function as reactive instincts be dangerously impaired but their particular function in the service of libidinal drives would be jeopardised. Even so a clinical distinction should be drawn between recognised fusions such as anal-sadism and instinct drives in which the destructive or libidinal aims respectively dominate.

If arguments concerning regression are to be based on the study of instincts which, clinically regarded, represent an important fusion, the question of the *specific* influence of aggressive and of libidinal components respectively must obviously be begged. Indeed it is interesting to observe that the authors are careful to preserve a "heads I win, tails you lose " system throughout their argument. Despite their emphasis on aggression factors they are careful to emphasise the element of fusion with libido. By so doing they provide themselves with a convenient avenue of escape should their favoured thesis become inconvenient. Anxiety, they say, arises from (is a primary reaction to) aggression. This statement is then carefully hedged : " It is evoked by the aggressive *components* (my italics) in the pre-genital stages of development " (whether these are independent components or fused components is left to the imagination). Anyhow they go on to say that further anxiety can be evoked by libidinal frustration and consequent further anxiety and hate. Incidentally it seems curious that libidinal energies, which, according to the authors have such effective power that they can neutralise the alleged all-important forces of aggression, which are (again according to the authors) the primary stimulus to anxiety, cannot apparently give rise to primary anxiety when frustrated. It is true the authors go on to say that regression is due *"not only"* to libidinal frustration, *"but also"* to hate, aggression and consequent anxiety. But in view of the persistent emphasis on aggression and the Death-Instincts, this reservation does not seem to have much practical value.

But after all the pragmatic test of a metapsychological theory is its application to *clinical* psycho-analysis. And in the clinical sense, this paper is more subversive of Freudian teaching than the two preceding papers. Its tendency is to ascribe a predominating influence in mental development to destructive and defensive systems; i.e., to negative reactive factors; for the authors have apparently little interest in the constructive force lent by the instincts of mastery when these are placed at the service of object-libido. The theory that fixation is a reaction to aggression is merely a special illustration of this main Kleinian viewpoint which ascribes to the destructive instincts some of the characteristics and tendencies Freud ascribed to the libido. For if fixation can be regarded as a reaction to (result of) aggression, and if regression itself works backwards through a developmental aggression series, it follows that progression must be attributed to the same factors. Indeed from the very beginnings of Kleinian theory its author has held this view. The Oedipus (i.e., libidinal) complex of the sixth month is, according to Klein, *released* by oral *sadism*. But what then becomes of the psycho-biological theory of the Life Instincts? What has happened to Freud's libido theory of neurosogenesis?

The answer is, of course, that it has been overlaid and stifled by the sheer weight of the Klein phantasy system. The fact is—and I have never seen why the Kleinians didn't continue to admit it joyfully, as indeed they did in the first and second stages of Klein theory—that they have developed an *entirely new* theory of neurosogenesis. In terms of this new theory, the classical Oedipus factor in neurosogenesis *must* be regarded as secondary or even tertiary. It isn't enough to say that the Kleinians have simply displaced backwards to early stages, the situations Freud placed at the age of 3—5 years. They certainly have done so in the case of the phantasy-systems of reparation which Freud placed in a late (obsessional) pre-genital phase and which Klein now places in the centre of an alleged depressive position occurring in the first months of life. But they have done more; they have, as Riviere explicitly maintained, based all psycho-pathology on oro-phallic sadistic phantasies and introjections alleged to occur in the first months of life. In the process the Freudian conception of regression has, as Friedlander put it, "vanished into thin air."*

(d) *"Depressive Position."* To those who were familiar with the earlier and more flamboyant phases of the Klein system, the fourth and last paper of the Controversial Series came as something of an anticlimax. In the days when the oro-phallic super-ego of the sixth month was all the rage, it seemed to me that nothing would ever discipline the imagination of the Klein Group. In papers and discussions both adherents and principals would produce all sorts of complicated "interpretations" prefaced merely with the sanctioning phrase "as Melanie Klein has shown" (or "come to see"). Yet it would appear that the overt criticism of the last ten years, together with the detailed

---

* Discussion. January, 1944. See also Hoffer (*Ibid*) for a comparison of the clinical systems of Freud and Klein.

examination of the Isaacs-Heimann (Klein) papers brought about a change in the method of presentation if not in the content of the last paper. By comparison with her earlier papers on ego development and with her original papers on the depressive position, Klein's paper on "The Emotional Life and Ego-development of the Infant with Special Reference to the Depressive Position"* is much more subdued in tone. But perhaps this may have been due to the facts that already the majority of her controversial opinions had been advanced by Isaacs and Heimann and that her restatement of theories of a depressive position was interspersed with a good deal of more general argument. Thus she is at pains to find in the work of Freud and of Abraham on anxiety, guilt, object formations, etc., quotations which she holds prove that her own views on phantasy, aggression, internal objects, etc., are extensions of their lines of thought. She includes also a lengthy discussion of the affective states which she assumes to exist in the infant and reviews the significance of early feeding difficulties, in terms which imply that behavouristic data all prove the accuracy of her metapsychological assumptions. To these points I will return. In the meantime it is necessary to summarise the passages in her description of the depressive position (which, it will be remembered, was one of the main points of controversy) which amplify or clarify earlier statements of this particular hypothesis.

Starting with "the strong and emotional relation to the mother *as a person* (my italics), which can be clearly observed from at least the beginning of the second month," she proceeds to say of genital impulses, "I think it possible that even from the beginning they influence, however dimly, the relation to objects." " We can assume that love towards the mother in some form exists from the beginning of life." "It is obviously *still more fundamental* that, when he becomes separated from his mother at birth, the infant who was at one with her feels her to be his first main love object." "One may assume that from the beginning the mother exists as a whole object in the child's mind but in vague outline as it were. . . ." Turning then to the infant's feelings of anxiety and guilt which, she believes originate from sadistic impulses and phantasies, she goes on to describe the infant's mental fear of loss of the love object "But the ego experiences it as a psychic reality that the loved object has been devoured, or is in danger of being devoured and therefore the loss of the love-object is the immediate consequence of these Cannibalistic desires." And (lest there should be any doubt about the date of these events) " the infantile depressive position arises when the infant perceives and introjects the mother as a whole person (between three and five months). The fear lest she be destroyed by his cannibalistic desires and phantasies gives rise to guilt." "However, the assumption seems justified that the seeds of depressive feelings, in so far as the experience of birth gives rise to a feeling of loss are there from the beginning of life." "My experience showed me that depressive feelings arise in infants, and that these feelings originate in early introjective processes." To repeat : " *The infant experiences feelings akin to mourning and those feelings arise from his fear of destroying and so losing his loved and indispensable object (as an external as well as an introjected object) through his Cannibalistic desires and through his greed.*"(Author's italics). "Defences against greed are possibly the earliest of all." "I suggest that the depressive

---

* Controversial Series IV. March, 1944.

position in infancy is a universal phenomenon." Standing, crawling, and walking " help the infant to overcome the depressive position." "The co-ordination of functions and of movements is bound up with a defence mechanism which I take to be one of the fundamental processes in early development, namely, the manic defence. This defence is closely linked with the depressive position and implies a control over the internal world."

Future generations of psycho-analytical students, looking over the files of the Klein controversy—and I think it is important that students should study the history of early deviations from psycho-analysis—will have little difficulty in recognising that the Controversial Series ended in a wild-goose chase. The whole series turned on the validity of Klein phantasies and on the concept of a central depressive position based in part anyhow on Klein phantasies. Yet at no point was any serious attempt made to establish the validity of the Klein interpretations. All the way through they were simply taken for granted and when the moment arrived to establish the "depressive position," that too was taken for granted. The reader was referred back to Klein's earlier papers on the subject. Apart therefore from the few quotations given above it is not possible to determine accurately how the original hypothesis of the depressive position had been getting on in the intervening ten years. Nevertheless, the paper is worth study, if only to follow the author's processes of thought.

The first point that strikes the reader is the baffling nature of the presentation. This is due not solely to the endless repetitions and paraphrasings which characterise most of Klein's writings, but also to the fact that the author cannot tell a developmental story straight, and so adds to the confusion inherent in her own metapsychological theories. Take, for example her views on object-formation. These are complicated by the fact that the author has to run two theories simultaneously; on the one hand the theory that shortly after birth the infant can "love" the mother as a "person" or a "whole" object, and on the other that primitive object formations are "part-objects" or "organ-objects" capable of immediate introjection; as witness, the introjection of "good" and "bad" breasts. What exactly constitutes the instinctual reference to the "whole" object is not clear even to the author. Klein thinks it may be an oral (breast) reference or a genital reference, the genital interests of the infant operating from birth through oral (breast) relations and so giving rise to "love" of the whole. Anyhow, there isn't much time to make up one's mind. For the depressive position implying the existence of a "whole" object starts at the third month and the attachment to a whole object already at the beginning of the second month. But, says Klein, rudiments of "whole" love also exist from birth. So there is no reason why the depressive position should not start from birth. And that I really believe is what Klein is driving at, for she links the depressive reaction of the infant to the birth trauma. Anyhow we soon get into difficulties with the Kleinian "psychic-reality" system, for apparently although the infant applies "psychic" reality to the breast situation (i.e., it interprets, or according to Riviere misinterprets, the situation in terms of feeling-phantasies), the infant seems to react to the whole object in a manner that is extremely reminiscent of an adult's reaction to external reality. And this means in turn that secondary processes involving reality perceptions and conscious reactions, are more readily applied to the "whole" object (the person) than to the "part"-object (the breast). Whereas I should have said that if there is anything in the Klein phantasy theory the exact reverse should be the case. Then again as regards the feeling of loss or fear of loss of the object, I defy any careful reader of this paper to be certain when this is a part-object loss or a whole-object loss. Sometimes it is one, sometimes the other, sometimes both, as when the cannibalistic impulses of the infant (which imply a part object (breast) reference) are held responsible for the infant's alleged belief that he has devoured the whole. And incidentally for all practical Kleinian purposes, cannibalistic means oral *sadistic, aggressive* impulses, despite Abraham's patent definition of them in terms of the *libido*. Indeed, it is interesting to note that whereas in the early Klein papers the early ego is an oro-phallic ego, in the present paper, despite a few cursory references to genital libido, it is clearly an oral ego. The cannibalistic sadistic phantasies are throughout concerned with the breast and its introjections. The real truth of the matter is that Klein made three cardinal blunders in these attempts at hypothetical reconstruction; first, to lay exclusive emphasis on an oro-phallic ego, subsequently scaling this down to an oral ego; second, and despite reference in earlier papers to anal components, to exclude in effect, all other libidinal components; and third, to compress all her theories of development into the concept of a unified ego. If the whole object is formed at the beginning of the second month and can be introjected as such, the primitive ego must have a unified and organised structure, for the unity of the ego is bound up with the existence of "whole" objects. True, Klein talks about rudimentary phases of object formation, but at the same time believes that from birth onwards rudimentary whole objects exist. Had she been ready to accept the nuclear theory of ego development, she might have avoided in part the bundle of contradictions with which she saddled her own metapsychology—but she didn't, possibly because it would have cut the ground from her theory of a *central* depressive position as well as from her theory that all mental disorders are derived from this position. For although in this paper she refers only to the fixation points of the psychoses and to the psychotic significance of early phobias, the famous Riviere footnote* on neurosogenesis still stands unaltered.

The same confusion between rudimentary and complex psychic manifestations occurs in her description of the affects alleged to be experienced by the infant. In an early paper on the nature of affects, I have indicated the necessity of closer differentiation of affects, in particular the distinction between primary affects and later fused affects, between affects that are characteristic of different states of instinct excitation (tension and discharge affects) and reactive affects that are secondary to traumatic states of tension. The later fusion of affects goes hand in hand with the development of more complicated forms of object relationship. By a sweeping simplification which is at the same time merely a sweeping assertion, Klein postulates "love" feelings for a "whole" object practically from the beginning of life. Similarly with feelings of loss, grief, and depression, the two to three months old infant is saddled with affects of a sophisticated nature which presuppose complicated object formations. And despite frequent references to early anxieties and to hypothetical guilt-feelings, the total result of the Klein formulations on infantile affect is to weaken rather than strengthen the basic

---

* See page 15.

concept of an anxiety response to danger situations of over-excitation. This weakening of Freud's concept of anxiety is increased by the concentration of Kleinian interest on oral impulse to the neglect of other instinctual components that are capable of evoking anxiety responses.

Nevertheless the parts of Klein's paper where she deals with infantile affects and with affective interpretation of the behaviour of sucklings are in one sense the most illuminating of all. The author evidently regards them as important pieces of evidence in support of her theories. Whereas in fact they merely go to show that Klein cannot imagine the infant's feelings in any psychic situation without injecting into them not only her own knowledge as an observer, but her own emotional bias. Thus, speaking of the infant's reaction when his smile is not responded to, she says, "The smile disappears, the light fades from his eyes, and something akin to sorrow and anxiety creeps into his expression." Or again referring to situations where the mother leaves the room "a fleeting expression of sadness came into the child's eyes." And again referring to the return of the mother, "Her very presence and signs of love re-establish the infant's belief in her as an unharmed and loving mother. This implies that his trust in his good internal and external objects increases and his fear of persecution by bad objects decreases." Some years ago M. Schmideberg* criticised the tendentious nature of the Klein interpretations, both of the infant's reactions and of environmental influences, and certainly if we were to string together the interpretations of the infantile situation given in this paper, we would be entitled to assume that infancy is a state in which loving mothers do nothing but love their babies, while babies alternate between loving their mothers and being very sad and depressed because they have destroyed them not merely in the real world, but in their own bodies and in their own minds. Now this is more than a gross over-idealisation of the mother's behaviour. It is a process of mother-justification which can be simply expressed in this formula : " If babies are sad, and fundamentally they are sad, it is their own fault : the real mother is good." If this adult formula is to be taken as a scientific assessment of infant mentality we may well ask whether the Klein theory of "psychic-reality," meaning the infant's misinterpretation of reality situations in terms of unconscious feeling-phantasy, could not be applied with profit to the scientific activities of adult observers of child life. Admittedly it is a welcome change to have some evidence brought regarding the method and tendency of interpretation on which the Klein theories are based but *no behaviouristic interpretations are worth the paper they are written on that do not include an objective assessment of the actual (ambivalent) behaviour of the mother during the infancy of the child.*

However absurd the results of these behaviouristic studies may have been, they served one useful purpose. One of A. Freud's criticisms of the Isaacs (Klein) phantasy concept was that it involved the operation in the unconscious mind of "secondary processes." To which I added that the phantasies as described were evidently derived from unconscious, pre-conscious and conscious mental systems. This view is strongly supported by the content of the last Klein paper. Hypothetical interpretations of infantile phantasy and mechanisms are interwoven with behaviouristic descriptions of the infant's reactions to external objects and of the development of reality estimations. Once this

---

* *Op cit.*

interweaving is disentangled the different methods of approach stand out clearly, each with a different relation to consciousness. Even so, on many occasions it is left uncertain whether the alleged feelings of the infant are conscious or unconscious. Indeed, it is interesting to note that with every step towards behaviouristic corroboration of Klein theory, the previous (Isaacs-Klein) concept of "psychic reality" is weakened, since in some of the behaviouristic studies the infant's feelings are regarded as reality estimates whereas according to the "psychic reality" hypothesis they ought to be phantasy misinterpretations. Indeed, some of Klein's behaviouristic descriptions sound as if the infant itself had, unwittingly, repudiated the Kleinian view that reality thinking is derived from an earlier phase of pure phantasy thinking. A similar confusion is to be noted in connection with the theory of a phase of "manic defence" supposed, as indeed the words "defence" and "position" imply, to follow the depressive position. The denial of reality associated with this phrase does not appear to differ from the denial implicit in the "psychic reality" of early phantasies. If this be so, the main feature of the "defence" appears before the "depressive position," not after it.

Now since the whole of the hypothetical system under survey is in a state of confusion and condensed over-simplification, these seeming modifications or retractions of earlier viewpoints are not very important in themselves. But they throw an interesting light on the earlier formulations. In the earlier Klein papers the starting point of theory was the development of an Oedipus situation at the sixth month. And this expressly involved an organised genital system with appropriate phantasies. No doubt the author could maintain that this is still her view but it is at least significant that the whole of the system described in this last paper is presented in oral terms and presumably therefore can stand without genital elements. Perhaps we are about to witness a swing away from the first year Oedipus theories : although personally I imagine both views will be maintained concurrently. And here is an appropriate point at which to comment on the more recently developed policy of the Klein Group, namely to shew that Freud held views which positively support Kleinian assumptions or that his theories were moving in directions that have been logically extended by Klein and her adherents. In the case of the Rank deviation from psycho-analysis, Freud was content to allow a year or so to elapse before he published any rebuttal of Rank's Birth Theory of Neurosogenesis. And when he did so it was in a casual manner almost as an after-thought. The few relevant paragraphs occurred in a monograph in which he clarified his own views on anxiety and sympton formation.* In the case of the Klein system, repudiation came almost from the first from the Vienna Psycho-Analytical Society, a branch of the International Psycho-Analytical Association in closest contact with Freud's views. But Freud himself apart from privately expressed comment did not trouble to take part in the Klein controversy. In one particular instance, however, when reviewing current theories of sexual development in childhood, he

---

* "Inhibition, Symptom and Anxiety."

did not disguise his rejection of the Klein position on this subject.* It is of course natural that when the Klein Group are taxed with major deviations from Freudian theory, they should respond by going through Freud's writings with a fine-tooth comb to garner sentences which, deprived of their context, appear to lend support to the Kleinian chain of reasoning. Yet it is interesting to observe that this alleged support is either the result of a preliminary interpretation made by the Kleinian scrutators or simply a *non-sequitur* directly appended to the quotation. I should have thought that if anything is clear from a survey of Freud's writings on mental development it is that the Kleinian ideology was quite alien to his psycho-biological outlook.

It remains to record the reactions of the so-called " Middle-Group "† throughout this Controversial Series of Discussions. Active part in the discussion was taken by three members of this Group, Brierley, Payne and Sharpe. The contributions of Payne and Sharpe were on the whole based on clinical, those of Brierley or metapsychological considerations. It is perhaps sufficient to summarise their reactions to the last paper.§ Payne's criticism was the most astringent, Sharpe's the mildest. Payne stressed the primary importance of archaic sexual impulses in the manifestations described as the depressive position. She also stressed the necessity of distinguishing between unorganised and organised forms of affect or ego structure and complained of the habit of using the same terms to designate different stages. But on the cardinal issue of the existence of a depressive position she temporised with the help of the phrase " as described by Klein."

Sharpe committed herself to an elaborate psychic content during the first year, but with a different stress on reality estimations. Amongst these she included " Accurate *perceptions* of reality that include the difference between the parent's genitals, awareness of what is going on between the parents, awareness when the mother becomes pregnant, the precursors of the Oedipus complex, repression of accurate perceptions, and so the precursors of super-ego formation. Phantasy formations are inseparable both from inner urges and the reality impacts. So far I confirm Mrs. Klein's data." One is left to infer that she disagrees on all other counts, including possibly the " depressive position," although she does speak of a " nucleus of

---

* The actual passage occurs in a paper on "Female Sexuality" (International Journal of Psycho-analysis, 1932, iii, 295). Referring to a paper by Fenichel on the pre-genital antecedents of the Oedipus complex Freud said: "He (Fenichel) ——— protests against Melanie Klein's displacement backwards of the Oedipus complex, whose beginnings she assigns to the commencement of the second year of life. This view of the date of origin of the complex, which in addition necessitates modification of our view of all the rest of the child's sexual development, is in fact not in accordance with what we learn from the analyses of adults and is especially incompatible with my findings as to the long duration of the girl's pre-Oedipal attachment to her mother. This contradiction may be softened by the reflection that we are not as yet able to distinguish in this field between what is rigidly fixed by biological laws and what is subject to change or shifting under the influence of accidental experience. We have long recognised that seduction may have the effect of hastening and stimulating to maturity the sexual development of children, and it is quite possible that other factors operate in the same way: such, for instance, as the child's age when brothers or sisters are born or when it discovers the difference between the sexes, or, again, its direct observation of sexual intercourse, its parents' behaviour in evoking, or repelling its love, and so forth." It will be observed that the date in question is the beginning of the second year. Later Klein specified the sixth month of life. It is not clear from her last paper how much earlier the Klein version of the Oedipus complex appears, but the depressive position is said to originate at the third month of life, relations to whole objects at the second month and genital elements from birth: so the reader is free to draw his own conclusion on the matter.

† This description was first applied to members of the British Society who held that some compromise could be arrived at between Freudian and Kleinian systems. As I have described in an earlier footnote, my original reactions to the first phase of Kleinian theory were in the direction of compromise. With the development of the second phase I entered into opposition. But a few members then took up the task I had abandoned and so qualified for the designation of Middle Grouper.

§ Discussion, March 1st, 1944.

depression." This she says is caused by growing awareness of rivals, the discovery of the father-mother relationship, their sexual differences or expected new child; situations which I venture to assert scarcely arise at the third month of life which is the date of emergence of Klein's depressive position. So one must assume that in this respect at any rate Sharpe is neither a Middle Grouper nor a Kleinian, but an orthodox Freudian.

Brierley's criticisms although couched in the most tentative of terms were in a sense the most uncompromising. Regarding the " depressive position " she says, " I see nothing improbable in the suggestion that infants pass through earlier stages of development just as typical as the classical Oedipus stage." Yet : " My own difficulty is that depression in the adult involves so much more than purely oral revival." Admitting that an infantile psychosis may originate during or after weaning, she adds, " What is in question for me is whether the " depressive position," as described by Mrs. Klein, is not too limited and narrow a concept as regards dynamics alone " . . . we must keep clear in our minds the difference between a primary simple affect and the complicated emotional attitudes of later life." " It does not seem to me that Mrs. Klein herself distinguishes clearly enough between the relationship which she observes to exist between the infant and its mother and the infant's own subjective appreciation of this relationship." As regards psychic organisation she says " The words in which Mrs. Klein phrases her assumptions sound as if they implied a degree of cognitive discrimination as distinct from feeling and sensory awareness in the infant, which the condition of its nervous system alone would preclude."[*] On the whole, therefore Brierley ranges herself against the second phase of Klein theory.

---

[*] Here Brierley is referring to the date of development of binocular vision. Friedlander had already advanced a similar argument, viz., that the phantasies described by Klein involved a variety of perceptions, conceptual and abstract thinking during the first year of life, in complete contradiction to the anatomical and physiological knowledge of the development of the brain, during the first year of life. The reference is of course to the date of myelinisation of the white matter and of the development of the cortex. Discussion. March 17th 1943.

V
CONCLUSION.

Now it may be, indeed has been, argued that all this is a storm in a tea-cup, that even if the Klein system constitutes a major deviation from Freudian theory, this doesn't matter very much. In the long run it is said, scientific method and thinking will prevail. And it has been suggested that the criticisms of the Freudian Group imply that they favour a "closed" system of psycho-analytical thought. Now if the election of members of psycho-analytical Groups (which up to the present is the equivalent of an official Diploma to practise Psycho-analysis) followed the lines adopted by societies for the promotion of natural science, there might be something in the first argument. But it does not. The transferences and counter-transferences developing during training analysis tend to give rise in the candidate to an emotional conviction of the soundness of the training analyst's theories. So much so that concurrently with the Controversial Series, the Training Committee was instructed to report on, amongst other matters, the influence of Klein teaching or training. Here was a good opportunity to test the strength of the views held by the Middle Group. The proof of the pudding is in the eating. The practical upshot of the Committee's deliberations is that Kleinian training analysts, control analysts and lecturers are still officially recognised, and are represented on the Controlling Committee. This means that many candidates trained at the present time will for the next twenty-five years practice and themselves propagate the Kleinian precepts.

As for the second point, it is true that there have been fallow periods in the development of psycho-analysis, that its expansion was almost exclusively the work of Freud himself. But that does not imply the existence of a "closed" system. On the contrary, Freud's own development of psycho-analytic theories indicated an unusual capacity on his part to modify or extend them where the clinical evidence demanded modification or extension. The confusion here is due to lack of distinction between basic formulations and working hypotheses regarding matters of clinical research. It is often and loosely thought that because Freud, for example, made important changes in his views on traumatic experiences or on the relation of the libido to anxiety, his basic formulations on the mental apparatus were equally subject to major modification. Nothing could be further from the truth. Freud clung with tenacity to his basic formulations regarding mind and was justified by events. He measured deviations from psycho--analysis by the degree to which their sponsors abandoned fundamental principles. It is no more true to say that Freud was ready to abandon his basic conceptions than to say that because cardiologists may change their clinical assessments or theories of heart disease, they are ready to abandon their belief in the circulation of the blood.

I do not intend to recapitulate here the list of Kleinian deviations I have set out in this review. They can be summed up as follows: first, by their definitions of phantasy the Klein Group have reduced to complete confusion the basic Freudian concepts of the mental apparatus and have opened the door to a mystical interpretation of life immediately after birth; second, in their outline of the development of instincts, mental mechanisms and ego structure, they have departed from the

Freudian tneory of the libido and have undermined the basic distinctions between unconscious, pre-conscious and conscious systems; third, by their theories of the " uninterrupted influence " of the first three to five months of life and by their alteration of the concepts of fixation and regression, they have abandoned the Freudian theory of neurosogenesis. If ever there was a " closed " system it is surely the Kleinian theory of a central depressive position developed between the third and fifth month of life. Not only does it run in direct contradiction to Freudian theories of neurosogenesis but if accepted, it would arrest all possibility of correlating the normal and abnormal manifestations of adult life with stages of development in infancy. It subverts all our concepts of progressive mental development from the unorganised to the organised.

But it is perhaps more interesting to consider what manner of deviation the Klein system constitutes. I have suggested before that particularly as regards neurosogenesis it resembles most closely the Rank "Birth Theory" deviation. Instead of Rank's birth trauma, we have offered as a "love trauma" of the third month, which, it is maintained, is as fateful for subsequent development as Rank thought the birth trauma to be. I imagine, however, that the Klein system is not simply an attempt to find new explanations for the clinical data of psycho-analysis, but that it owes its existence also to some urge towards a new *Weltanschauung*, together with a natural desire to bridge the gap in our reconstruction of life between the intra-uterine and the extra-uterine state. *In my considered opinion the concept of a three-months-old love-trauma due to the infant's imagined greedy destruction of a real loving mother whom it really loves is merely a matriarchal variant of the doctrine of Original Sin.*

CPSIA information can be obtained at www.ICGtesting.com
Printed in the USA
LVOW082155290911

248507LV00001B/150/P

9 781446 522509